The Moon & I

The first time I owned a snake I was 7 years old, and the snake was mine for about fifteen glorious minutes.

Back then I didn't want to be a writer. I didn't know any writers—I had never even seen one—but their photographs looked funny, as if they'd been taken to a taxidermist and stuffed.

I read a lot, so I saw many dust-jacket photographs, and it seemed to me that no matter how hard authors tried—the men put pipes in their mouths and the women held little dogs—nothing helped. Authors, even my favorites, looked nothing like the kind of person I wanted to become.

This corpselike look, I figured, came from sitting alone all day in a room typing, which couldn't be good for you. Oh, sure, I was glad there were people willing to do this. I loved books and didn't want them to become extinct. But I cared too much about myself and my future to consider becoming one of them.

When I grew up I was going to work in a zoo.

BETSY BYARS

The Moon and I

A Beech Tree Paperback Book
New York

This edition is reprinted by arrangement with Simon & Schuster Books for Young Readers,
Simon & Schuster Children's Publishing Division.
Inquiries should be addressed to
Simon & Schuster, 1230 Avenue of the Americas, New York, NY 10020.
Printed in the United States of America.

HarperCollins Children's Books, a division of HarperCollins Publishers,
195 Broadway, New York, NY 10007

Library of Congress Cataloging in Publication Data
Byars, Betsy Cromer.
The moon and I / by Betsy Byars. p. cm.
Summary: While describing her humorous adventures with a blacksnake, Betsy Byars recounts
childhood anecdotes and explains how she writes a book.
1. Byars, Betsy Cromer—Biography—Juvenile literature.
2. Authors, American—20th century—Biography—Juvenile literature. 3. Children's stories—
Authorship—Juvenile literature. 4. Snakes—Anecdotes—Juvenile literature. [1. Byars, Betsy
Cromer. 2. Authors, American. 3. Women—Biography 4. Authorship. 5. Snakes.] 1. Title.
[PS3552.Y37Z47 1996] 813'.54—dc20 95-53100 CIP AC
ISBN 0-688-13704-0

Originally published in 1991 by Julian Messner, a division of Simon & Schuster
First Beech Tree Edition, 1996

16 BR 20 19 18 17

CONTENTS

ONE

A Snake Named Moon

I glanced up and saw it.

Snake, I said to myself. That looks like a snake.

I got up out of my porch rocking chair and went closer.

That *is* a snake.

I stopped moving closer.

The snake lay on an overhead beam. It was long and slender. It was doubled back over its body, its head pillowed on one of its loops. The snake was so dark in color, it looked black. The eyes were round, the stare unblinking—and the round, unblinking eyes were looking at me.

I had been sitting on the porch for an hour, editing one of my books, and for an hour this snake had been watching me.

Now I don't like anybody watching me when I'm writing—particularly snakes.

I can't even write when my dog's watching. My dog can lie

1

down under the word processor and sleep—that's fine, but when he starts watching, I can't write. I have to say, "Want to go for a *walk*?" *Walk* and *sup-per* are my dog's favorite words. I can't keep saying, "Want *sup-per*?" or the dog would end up weighing a thousand pounds.

Here's the way I write a book:

• I start on the word processor and write as much as I can. Then I print it.

• I take what I've printed, go sit somewhere else—like the porch—read it, say, "This is terrible," and start working on it.

• I go back to the word processor, put in the changes, and print it.

• I take what I've printed, go sit somewhere else, say, "Oh, this is *still* terrible," and rewrite it.

• I keep doing this until I say, "This is not as terrible as it used to be," then, "This is getting better," and finally (hopefully), "This is not bad at all."

That's how I do my writing, no matter what kind it is—short stories, essays, novels. And it's worked for thirty years.

So, I was on the porch saying, "This is *still* terrible," when I looked up and saw this snake coiled high on one of the beams.

I moved my rocking chair back a bit. If the snake dropped off the beam, it could land on my lap. Nobody wants a lapful of snake.

I settled down to watch.

The snake continued to lie in its relaxed coil. It shifted position occasionally—stretching out full length, recoiling, curving, but it never moved from the beam.

I didn't know much about snakes, but the color—black— was comforting. Blacksnakes are harmless and beneficial. They go after mice, which I had a few of and which they were welcome to.

This snake was obviously not on the prowl at the moment. It might even be digesting one of my mice.

Slowly the snake raised its head, and I saw the startling milky white of the chin and throat. I decided to call my husband for a second opinion.

"Yes, it's a blacksnake," Ed confirmed.

"But the throat is white. Are you sure blacksnakes have white throats?"

"Yes."

"Blacksnakes don't . . . er . . . bite, do they?"

"They can."

"Oh."

"But their bite is never more than a scratch."

"Ah."

I was gaining confidence.

"If cornered, the blacksnake will put up a good front," he went on. "It will even shake its tail like a rattler, but it's not a good fighter. Sometimes it becomes so frantic it bites its own body."

That was my kind of snake.

There was a pause while my husband and I admired the snake, and the snake allowed us to.

"Have you got a heavy plastic garbage bag?" my husband asked abruptly.

"Garbage bag? What do you want a garbage bag for?"

"I think I'll take the snake to the airport," Ed said. His hangar at the airport was troubled by mice.

My reaction was instant and protective. "You can't have it," I said, "It's mine."

Meeting a snake on my front porch had been a pleasant distraction, and I like distractions—especially when I'm writing.

After a while, however, I went back inside to the word processor. The window in the room where I work faces out onto the porch, and I got up frequently to check on what was now "my snake."

The snake was always there, but its position changed every time I looked. Sometimes the snake was draped around the beam like a scarf. Sometimes the snake's tail dangled below. Sometimes the head was tucked out of sight, under the body. Whatever the position, it was graceful and pleasing to watch.

As the afternoon wore on, my snake checks became more frequent. I didn't think the snake would spend the night on the porch, and I wanted to see where it went after it left. I wanted to see it slither down the wisteria vine—which was probably how it got up on the porch in the first place—and I wanted to see where it went.

Then something happened to me. I became totally engrossed in what I was writing.

Now most of the time I plod along, writing word by word, sentence by sentence. But then sometimes, suddenly—it's like switching to a higher gear in a car—I take off.

That's what happened now—I took off. I wrote furiously for about an hour. It was as if an invisible dam had burst, and my fingers on the keyboard could barely keep up with my mind.

It was six o'clock when the magical flow stopped. My thoughts immediately returned to the snake, and I jumped up and went to the window.

The snake was gone.

Of all the stupid things to do—I had let my writing get in the way of my snake watching!

Disappearances upset me—*a lot*.

I felt exactly like I did the time I left my word processor for less than a minute—one minute!—and I discovered when I got back that the chapter I had been working on had disappeared!

An entire chapter had vanished!

Later, when I was more rational, I figured up exactly how long I was away from the word processor. Here are my calculations:

Walk to refrigerator .... 11 seconds
Take miniature Snickers from freezer .... 3 seconds
Warm Snicker in microwave .... 16 seconds
Return eating Snicker .... 11 seconds
Total elapsed time .... 41 seconds

And in forty-one seconds a whole chapter disappeared! Vanished! To this day I don't know where that chapter went!

And that chapter was perfect! It was the only perfect chapter I have ever done in my life!

And now, instead of a perfect chapter, I had a blank screen! I freaked.

I started pressing keys. I paged up. I paged down. I punched escape (which I had been saving to punch when I was truly desperate). I punched home, end, scroll, control, F1, F2, F3 ... AF1, AF2 ...

You name it, I punched it.

My last desperate punch was AF10. Then I stored.

UNDER WHAT NAME?

BS (BS stood for Blank Space because subconsciously I knew even then that was what I was storing.)

FILE STORED ON DISK. YOUR CHOICE?

RETRIEVE

WHICH FILE?

BS

I waited with my heart in my throat only to have my worst fears realized. I had indeed stored—and I now retrieved—a blank space.

At that point I did the only sensible thing left to do. I turned off the word processor and went back to the refrigerator for another miniature Snickers.

(Actually, it's no wonder I don't want anybody watching me write.)

Now it was the same thing all over again. I had had a perfect snake. Now I had a blank space. And worst of all, I didn't even have a retrieve key to press.

TWO

E!G!G!S!

The first time I owned a snake I was 7 years old, and the snake was mine for about fifteen glorious minutes.

Back then I didn't want to be a writer. I didn't know any writers—I had never even seen one—but their photographs looked funny, as if they'd been taken to a taxidermist and stuffed.

I read a lot, so I saw many dust-jacket photographs, and it seemed to me that no matter how hard authors tried—the men put pipes in their mouths and the women held little dogs—nothing helped. Authors, even my favorites, looked nothing like the kind of person I wanted to become.

This corpselike look, I figured, came from sitting alone all day in a room typing, which couldn't be good for you. Oh, sure, I was glad there were people willing to do this. I loved books and didn't want them to become extinct. But I cared too much about myself and my future to consider becoming one of them.

When I grew up I was going to work in a zoo. I would take care of the baby animals whose mothers had rejected them. I envisioned myself in an attractive safari outfit feeding lion cubs and other exotic offspring from a bottle.

In preparation for this life my best friend, Wilma, and I played "Zoo" a lot. This consisted of setting up zoos in the backyard and begging people to come and view the exhibits.

The bug exhibit was always the largest but drew the least attention. Ants, doodlebugs, beetles went unacclaimed—even lightning bugs since the zoo was not open at night and their daytime "thing" was resting on the underside of leaves.

Tadpoles (in season) were a popular exhibit, especially when the legs started coming out. Slugs had a certain "yuck" appeal, as did leeches (which we got by wading in a forbidden creek and pulling them off our ankles).

Butterflies were popular, but also seasonal, and the favorite exhibits were the snails and box turtles, which, in addition, required little maintenance.

Admission was free.

Wilma and I were always on the alert for new acquisitions and went about regularly during the summer months turning over stones and rotten logs.

One July afternoon Wilma and I set out, followed by my goat Buttsy who liked to be in on things. While the three of us were rooting through the woodpile, we came across some eggs. The eggs were buried in the rotten sawdust at the bottom of the pile.

And these were not just eggs. These were E!G!G!S!

We said the word so many times with so many different inflections that it no longer sounded like a word but more like an inhuman cry of triumph.

The eggs were capsule-shaped, about two inches long, and leathery in appearance. There were about a dozen of them.

They weren't hard like hen's eggs but were elastic and tough. They were light in color—an almond white—and smooth.

These were really and truly E!G!G!S!

When we calmed down at last, a disagreement followed over what should be done with them.

There were three possibilities.

Wilma brought up the first. She would take them home with her.

I reminded Wilma of the violent reaction her mother had had to our trained cicadas.

This had happened one day when Wilma and I were training cicadas on her screen porch. This was with an eye to a future circus.

We would start the cicadas up the screen. When they were halfway up, we would tap the screen—sharply—and the cicadas would immediately turn around and go back down. That had been the extent of the training, but we had more complex tricks in mind.

"Get the bugs off the porch," Wilma's mother had said.

"Mom, they aren't bugs, they're cicadas."

"Get—the—bugs—off—the—porch."

"Mom, we're training them."

"Train them over at Betsy's house."

"We can't! Betsy doesn't have a screen porch!"

"Now!"

The second possibility—my own—was that I would take the eggs home with me.

Wilma reminded me of the violent reaction my mother had had to the leeches.

This happened the first time we came upon leeches and didn't know what they were. In our enthusiasm we ran up from the creek to show everybody the weird brown things on our ankles that didn't want to come off.

"Leeches!" my sister had cried in a way that let us know weird brown things were not a good thing to have on our ankles. "Mother, Betsy's got leeches on her ankles!"

My mother came out of the house, got a sharp stick and pried my leeches off. This hurt enough to make me cry. When Wilma heard my cries of pain, she quickly got her own sharp stick and pried hers off herself.

"I don't ever want to see you with leeches on your ankles again," my mother said with a shake of the leech stick.

"You won't," I answered, still tearful.

And she never did because Wilma and I pried the leeches off the minute we got out of the creek, before they had time to stick. The leech display, while not popular with adults, was one of our regulars.

The third, and less appealing possibility, was to leave the eggs where they were.

We compromised.

Wilma put two of the eggs and some sawdust in her mayonnaise jar—the holes were already in the lid. I put two of the eggs and some sawdust in my mayonnaise jar—ditto on the holes—and we left the rest in the woodpile.

The eggs stuck together a little bit, but we managed to get four separated without breaking anything—including our friendship.

"Be careful! Be careful!"

"I am being careful. You're the one who's not being careful."

The eggs weren't slimy, but they were moist, and Wilma and I promised to water ours faithfully.

We thought—hoped!—the eggs were snake eggs, but we agreed, like future parents, that we would not be the least disappointed in baby turtles.

Wilma's eggs never got the opportunity to hatch because

Wilma's sister said, "Motherrrr, Wilma put some funny-looking eggs in our sock drawerrrrr."

Wilma had three sisters and they all wore the same size socks and borrowed from each other, so this was not exactly a clever hiding place.

Wilma's mother promptly flushed her eggs down the toilet.

I hid my mayonnaise jar in the back of my closet. I checked my eggs often—like two hundred times a day.

About a week after I had put the mayonnaise jar behind my roller skates, one of the eggs looked different. It seemed to move. I took the jar to the window.

A slit appeared in the egg.

Fluid leaked out.

A small snout appeared.

"Everybody! Everybody! My egg is hatching!"

The hatching took about a day. The jar was allowed a place of honor in the center of the kitchen table, and we all watched—I with my chin resting on my hands, staring into the glass.

By the time the snake emerged—it took its time—the egg casing had been slashed to ribbons.

The snake was small—about six inches in length—and absolutely perfect. It was brownish. My father said it was a bullsnake.

My father held it in his hand and it crawled and twisted in a lively manner. Then I held it in my hand. It was like holding a strand of electrified brown spaghetti.

I dropped it and it got into a perfect striking position. Its tail shook.

My father said, "When a snake wags its tail at you, it's not being friendly."

After that my mother made me put the snake back in the

mayonnaise jar, take it out in the yard, and let it go.

"I want to keep it! I have to keep it! I'll take care of it myself! You won't have to do a thing! I'll keep the lid on the jar! I'll feed it and clean the cage and—"

"Now."

"Motherrrrrr. . ."

"Now!"

I released the baby bullsnake in the field beside our house. I watched it slither away into the tall grass with the painful, heart-breaking regret that only a 7-year-old who *needs* a snake can know.

Back then, one of the reasons I wanted to become an adult was so that I could have as many pets as I wanted.

My list was long. It started out:

• As many dogs as possible.

• At least two horses—male and female—and all of their colts.

• A goat exactly like my goat Buttsy (who had recently died and whom I missed every time I got in the hammock—Buttsy used to push me).

Now I added to the list:

• Pet snake, preferably nonpoisonous.

So when I saw the snake on my front porch that July afternoon, it was as if a childish dream, long forgotten, had come true at last.

And now the dream was gone!

THREE

The Missing Moon

I rushed out onto the porch. The first thing I checked was the wisteria vine. The twisting tentacles look enough like a snake to be one—no snake.

I checked the maple tree. The limbs touch the porch in a few places. A snake could possibly . . . if it knew exactly which limb to reach for . . . no snake.

I sat down in a rocker and sighed with disappointment.

And this snake had been perfect! It was the first perfect snake I had seen in fifty years and now it was gone! Vanished! This was worse than losing a chapter.

And, let's face it, a chapter can be rewritten. Maybe it won't be perfect, but it will be a chapter. Anyway, a chapter that was absolutely perfect might make the rest of the chapters look bad.

But with a snake . . .

I heard a noise.

I got up and glanced over the porch railing. There was the snake on the ground, cornered in an angle of the chimney. A neighbor's calico cat—Ginger—held it in place.

My heart actually leapt, like in poetry.

Thank you, Ginger.

Ginger and the snake were involved in a tense, eyeball-to-eyeball face-off.

The sounds I had heard were coming from the cat. These were low, throaty growls that couldn't have had much effect because snakes don't have ears.

The snake remained coiled, silent, alert, and ready. The tip of its tail began to quiver.

Perhaps, I thought, the snake was gearing up for one of those brave, absurd fights my husband had spoken of. I was torn between wanting to see the snake in action and not wanting to see it bite its own body.

Like a mother whose child is threatened, I slapped my hands against the side of the railing.

"Go home, Ginger!"

The cat looked up, startled. Then she dashed into the woods, taking the shortcut for home.

My snake remained for a moment, testing the climate with flicks of its dark, forked tongue. Then, apparently satisfied that the danger had passed, the snake began uncoiling.

The black color was startling against the green ivy, and I could see that the snake was longer than I had thought—about six feet.

The snake began to move in a series of graceful S-curves, its head a few inches off the ground.

It circled the chimney. The movement was as slick as mercury.

The chimney began to block the snake's path from my view,

and I wanted to see where it was going. I did not want another disappearance.

I rushed into the living room, dashed around the sofa, and threw open the sliding door to the back deck.

I went out and leaned over the railing, waiting . . . waiting . . .

The snake did not appear.

After a moment I accepted the fact that the snake was not going to appear. I walked down the steps, paused to check the path, and then walked slowly down the path. I was looking for a hole or a crevice where the snake could have disappeared.

No hole, no crevice . . . no snake.

Suspecting that the snake had been fast enough to get under the deck before I—with all my speed—could get to the deck, I knelt and peered through the dusty, late-afternoon sunlight.

No snake.

With a sigh I went back inside the house to turn off the word processor.

At the end of a writing day the last thing I do is take the pages I have completed, punch three holes in them, and fit them into a loose-leaf notebook.

I take this notebook home with me. I write at my log house, but I live about five minutes away in a condominium on Lake Hartwell. Sometimes I even get a flash of inspiration on the way home and pull over onto the side of the road to scribble.

This night I did no scribbling. My notebook remained closed. Snakes are much, much more interesting than manuscripts.

"Guess what?" I said to my grandson over the phone that night.

"What?"

"I have a pet snake!"

"Where did you get it?"

"It came up on my porch."

"Does it have a name?"

"Moon," I said, without missing a beat.

"Granny, Moon's not a good name for a snake."

"Yes, it is, because the first time I saw this snake, it was high over my head. And ever since then it's brought a nice glow to my life."

"Then Moon is a good name for a snake."

"And," I went on, "the reason I call it my 'pet' snake is not because I keep it in a cage or anything. The word *pet* means favorite. So this is my favorite snake. That's why I say it's my pet snake."

"I wish I had a pet snake."

"They are nice."

"I hope I'll get to see Moon sometime."

"I hope you will, too."

End of pet snake discussion.

And probably, I thought regretfully as I hung up the phone, end of Moon.

"Everyone is a moon," Mark Twain said, "and has a dark side which he never shows to anybody."

I didn't think of Mark Twain's quotation when I gave Moon that name, but it wouldn't be long before I would see its dark side.

FOUR

Mummy Hand and the Reptile Room

Speaking of dark sides, every time I had a character in my books that I didn't like I used to name him Bubba. And as soon as I typed the word *Bubba*, a chill of distaste would come over me and the character would spring to life. I never had any trouble creating a terrible character as long as his name was Bubba.

That's how important names are to me. The names have to be right or the characters won't come to life.

Like when I was writing *The Night Swimmers*, I had three characters and I named them George and Barbara and Henry, and they would not come to life. They just floated around in the swimming pool, getting waterlogged.

Their father's name was Shorty Anderson and he ran an all-night garage, and he wouldn't come to life either. Then, one night, I saw Little Jimmy Dickens on Grand Ole Opry, and I thought, why, Shorty Anderson is Little Jimmy Dickens! He's a country-western star! He would have named his kids for country-western stars! The girl would be Retta for Loretta Lynn! The boys would be Johnny and Roy for Johnny Cash and Roy Acuff! I was off and running.

Or when I was writing *The 18th Emergency,* I wanted the bully to be terrible. (At first I named him Bubba, of course, but this time it didn't really work.) This time I needed a name that nobody else in the world had.

I finally came up with Marv Hammerman because of the good hard sound of the name. I thought it was unique. In the book I used the line "There had only been one Hammerman, just as there had only been one Hitler."

After the book was published, the phone rang one day. A man said, "Is this Betsy Byars?"

I said, "Yes, who is this?"

He said, "Marv Hammerman."

I said, "Who is this really?" I thought it was someone playing a joke.

He said, "Marv Hammerman."

It turned out the name wasn't so unique. This Marv Hammerman was a teacher and he had started reading *The 18th Emergency* to his class. He said his class was delighted to find there were two terrible Marv Hammermans, and he took it very well!

Back to Bubba. I wasn't even aware I was using the name for every loathsome character I had until a reader said to me one day, "Mrs. Byars, you must have known someone you didn't like named Bubba."

I stopped for a moment, and the Bubba from my childhood rose in my mind the way monsters rise out of the slime in horror movies.

"Yes, I did," I answered.

Bubba lived on the same street as my grandparents in Charleston, South Carolina, where my family visited every summer. Bubba was smart, quick-witted, and mean—a bad combination. The thing I tried to do—where Bubba was concerned—was stay out of his way. I was best friends with his sister Louisa and she liked to stay out of his way, too.

This worked fine as long as Bubba was involved with his own activities, but when Bubba was at loose ends and bored—look out.

Louisa and I were going to the Charleston Museum one afternoon. The museum was about five blocks away. It was a big, roomy old museum that featured, surprisingly, a lot of Egyptian artifacts and a live reptile room.

Louisa and I were halfway to the museum when we realized Bubba was following. "Leave us alone," Louisa turned to say.

"I'm not bothering you. Am I bothering you?" Bubba lifted his hands innocently to show he was blameless.

As far as I was concerned, the museum trip, which I had looked forward to—I especially loved the mummy and the reptile rooms—was ruined.

At the end of the block we turned again. Bubba was still there.

"I'm going to tell Mama on you," Louisa said.

"Tell her what? Tell her I was walking down the sidewalk? This is a public sidewalk. If you think I'm following you and Loud Mouth,"—this was his cruel nickname for me—"you're even stupider than I thought you were."

At the museum entrance we turned in. Bubba turned in, too.

Before Louisa could speak, Bubba said, "It's a public building." Bubba had a sharp, weasel-like face, and when he opened his eyes to look innocent, he looked even more threatening.

Louisa and I entered the museum. It was early afternoon and hot. The small children who would later run through the huge building were home taking naps. Louisa and I—and Bubba—

pretty much had the place to ourselves.

Once we were inside the building we could no longer see Bubba, but we could hear him, slipping around the outskirts of the exhibits, hiding behind an old boat or stuffed polar bear, waiting to spring out at us.

We were steeled for the spring, certain he would jump out at the worst possible moment. That—as far as I was concerned— was at the mummy.

I had a sort of fascination with mummies, and since this was the only one I had ever seen—or was likely to see—it was special.

Bubba was there, waiting for us, leaning with deceptive ease against the glass case that enclosed the mummy. He looked from me to Louisa.

"You want to touch it?" Bubba asked.

Neither Louisa nor I spoke.

"Or are you scared?"

Bubba's greatest scorn was for those who were scared. When he spoke the word, it became a sneer. The key to Bubba, Louisa had told me, was not letting him know what you were scared of—like if he knew you were scared of frogs, he would drop one down the back of your shirt and playfully slap you on the back. "How're you doing?" Slap, slap. "Glad to see you." Slap, slap, *squishhhh*!

Louisa put her hands on her hips. "We aren't scared, and anyway I've already touched it and you know it."

"Loud Mouth hasn't," Bubba said, letting his hooded, weasel eyes settle on me.

"Well, she's not scared either, are you, Betsy?"

"No," I lied. The nickname Loud Mouth no longer fit because I could not speak above a whisper.

"Then she can touch it."

He beckoned me behind the mummy case, and I went. He lifted up the glass about an inch.

"Put your finger in."

"No," I said. "You'll drop the case down on my finger."

"Put your finger in, Stupid."

I put my finger in and touched the mummy. "There," I said.

"Did you really touch it or did you just fake it?"

"I really and truly, honestly touched it," I said.

Bubba's weasel expression turned to horror. "You touched it?"

"Yes, you told me to."

"You touched it?"

"Yes, wasn't I supposed to?"

"She touched it?" Bubba said, throwing out his thin arms. "Stupid, you don't touch it. You pretend to touch it. You know what happens if you really touch it, don't you?"

"No."

"Your hand, your whole hand will turn into a mummy hand."

"It will not."

"It will, too," Bubba said. "You just wait and see, and there's nothing you can do. You can't even go to the doctor and get a shot. You're going to be Mummy Hand. And then if you touch the rest of you with the mummy hand, it will—"

"Oh, Bubba, quit making up stuff," Louisa said.

"I didn't make it up," Bubba said. "It says right here"— Bubba turned to a stone with some hieroglyphics on it— "whatsoever hand shall touch the mummy shall become a mummy hand, and whatsoever that mummy hand shall touch shall become a mummy as well."

The "whatsoevers" gave the reading a Biblical, truthful ring that made me quiver. "I've got to go to the bathroom," I said.

I went into the bathroom and washed my hand hard. This wasn't easy because I had to do it one-handed—I couldn't touch the mummy hand with my other hand because whatsoever . . .

Finally I came out, smelling strongly of restroom soap. "I have to go home," I said.

"Not before we see the snakes," Louisa said. We always saved the reptile room for last. Both Louisa and I liked snakes.

We headed for the back of the museum and the reptile room where live alligators and snakes slept their lives away. The alligators were in a concrete pond and the snakes in glass cages. There were mostly local snakes—a couple of cottonmouths, which were incredibly ugly snakes, a couple of boas, water moccasins, rattlers.

We walked into the reptile room and I glanced without my usual interest at the occupants. I wanted to get home and put some iodine or alcohol or something on my hand. It was already beginning to feel dry.

The snakes were listless—curled into balls or coiled on rocks. Louisa and I were at the cottonmouth cage, marveling again at the ugliness, when behind us Bubba said, "Want to see them open their mouths?"

We were startled because he had come into the room as silently as a snake itself.

"It says right there"—Louisa pointed to a sign—"don't knock on the glass."

"I'm not going to knock on it. I'm going to slap on it." And Bubba slapped his long, thin hand against the glass of the cottonmouth cage.

The cottonmouths slept on.

Bubba rapped again, this time with his knuckles, and the snakes came alive. One struck at the glass, revealing the sickeningly pale inside of its mouth, the other pulled its short body into striking position. Its tail trembled a warning.

Bubba rapped with both hands now, one on one side of the cage, one on the other, causing the snakes to strike from side to side. "Hey, Stupids," Bubba said, "I'm over here . . . No, I'm over here . . . No, I'm over—"

Bubba never got to finish. The guard caught him from behind by the shoulder. "I thought I told you that you could never come back into the reptile room again."

Bubba's mouth fell open as he turned to face the guard.

"You remember that?"

Bubba shook his head dumbly.

"You were in here two months ago upsetting the snakes, and I barred you from the reptile room. Do you remember?"

The guard tightened his hold on Bubba's collarbone so hard that Bubba winced. "Now do you remember?"

Bubba nodded.

"I want you to leave the museum, and if I ever see you in the reptile room again, you won't even be allowed back in the museum. Is that clear?"

Bubba nodded.

"I know your mother, and I'll call her if I have to."

"You won't," Bubba said.

The guard released him. Bubba got as far as the door. Then he turned and sneered. "Anyway, I don't know why you're after *me, she's* the one who put her hand in the mummy case!"

Bubba pointed to me, and the guard turned in my direction.

"She did not put her hand in the mummy case," Louisa said loyally, "just one finger!"

"You kids behave yourselves," the guard said, tiredly. He left Louisa and me in the reptile room and saw Bubba to the door.

Louisa called after them, "And, Bubba, if you don't leave us alone from now on, I'm going to tell Mama on you."

The short-range results of the incident were these:

• Bubba did not leave us alone—though he never called me Mummy Hand again.

• The mummy case was sealed so that no other child could ever touch a real mummy.

The long-range result was this:

• I finally stopped using the name Bubba in my books, but when I want to create a character that I won't like and the reader won't either, I still think, Oh, I want this character to be something like . . . Bubba.

FIVE

Only a Cardboard Moon

The main characters of this book will be:

    1. A snake named Moon

    2. A writer named Betsy Byars

The time and setting will be:

    1. A log house (today)

    2. A rural neighborhood in Charlotte, N.C. (fifty years ago)

The plots will be:

    1. The writer, Betsy Byars, comes to know a snake, Moon, and blah . . . blah . . . blah . . . blah.

That is not the way I start a book. Here is the way I start a book:

THE MOON AND I

by

Betsy Byars

I typed those words one Thursday in July, the day after I first saw Moon. I didn't think I would actually write a book about a snake.

The truth is that I love to type title pages. I type them all the time. It makes me feel so good, so full of hope that I type many, many more title pages than I could ever use.

When I type a title page, I hold it and I look at it and I think, I just need four thousand sentences to go with this and I'll have a book!

The top drawer of my desk—which is where I keep things that I don't want to lose—is cluttered with loose title pages. I come across them as I flip through clippings and letters and photographs that I also don't want to lose.

Some title pages were typed on typewriters so old that the typescript is no longer familiar to me.

THE ONE-WAY CAVE by Betsy Byars.

MISS PINKERTON AND THE ORANGUTANG by Betsy Byars.

THE APRIL FOOLS by Betsy Byars.

THE MERMAID MIX-UP by Betsy Byars.

THE PINK ACE by Betsy Byars. (I do remember this one—it was going to be about an aviator pig.)

But with most of these titles, I can't even remember typing them, can't recall what I could possibly have had in mind.

It's as much a mystery as why I have kept a clipping about a man who ate thirty-nine watermelons or this photograph of two beagles in sombreros or this story about a woman who put her very old hamster into the freezer to give him a merciful death and the next morning found he had eaten through a box of french fries and was having a ball in a vegetable lasagna.

Anyway, there's no single moment in my life that is more satisfying, more full of promise for a bright and interesting future than a title page. It's a door about to be opened.

But there was another, stronger reason why I didn't want to write the book. Snakes had appeared as bad guys in two of my books. In *The TV Kid* a rattlesnake had bitten a boy named Lennie, and in *A Blossom Promise* another rattler bit a dog named Dump. The only person that could be bitten in this book was me.

That had no appeal at all.

Still, I began to do what I always do when I start a book. If I start a book about a fox, I read fox stories, fox articles, fox books. I want to know everything there is to know about a fox.

Even if the setting of the novel is familiar—like the beach—I start reading books about beaches. I read about them until I can actually feel the sand between my toes, though I'm sitting at home in the middle of January.

If the setting is unfamiliar—like the rodeo—I not only read about rodeos, I head west. I go to rodeos and I wear rodeo clothes and I eat rodeo food and I smell rodeo air and I keep a notebook in my lap and put down all these things so I won't forget them when I get home.

And if I'm writing a book that doesn't fit into any category—other than that it's contemporary fiction, which is what I write these days—then I read contemporary fiction, one book after another.

For me, reading books and writing them are tied together. The words of other writers teach me and refresh me and inspire me.

So the next day I went to the library and checked out three books on snakes. I looked up blacksnakes in the index and began reading charming stories.

Charming Story Number One:

There was this man who had a pet blacksnake. This man tied a dead mouse to a string and dangled it in front of the snake. The snake left its cage and followed the owner through the house. The owner went up a ladder into a loft. The snake went up right behind him. In the loft the owner stood like the Statue of Liberty and the snake slithered up his raised arm and took the mouse.

I loved that story. I wasn't sure I'd want a blacksnake slithering up my raised arm, but . . .

Charming Story Number Two:

There was this hunter who was going through the woods one day and he came across a tree. About twenty feet up in the tree was an opening where honeybees were leaving and entering. Draped near the opening was a blacksnake, and this blacksnake was snapping up the bees as they returned from gathering nectar.

This really was my kind of snake. I flipped through the books, looking for more charming stories, skipping the not-so-charming ones.

Not-So-Charming Story Number One:

There was this hunter who saw a blacksnake in a cotton field. The hunter chased the snake, and the snake disappeared into a crevice. Apparently the snake was unfamiliar with the crevice, which turned out to be only twelve inches deep. The blacksnake turned, reappeared, and in its frustration struck at the man again and again and again. The man reported he had never seen such fury in a snake.

Not-So-Charming Story Number Two:

There was this man who wanted to race a snake. He saw it heading for its hole, and he ran as fast as he could and got to the hole first and put his foot over the hole, and this made the snake so mad it jumped up and bit him on the cheek.

I also skipped Not-So-Charming Bits of Information, like:

A blacksnake can strike half the distance of its length.

This meant that, since Moon was about six feet long, Moon could strike from a distance of three feet. Or to put it in an even less charming way, Moon could strike at *me* from a distance of three feet.

If I had had that striking piece of information I would never have gotten within three feet of Moon's head.

So these stories of honeybees and ladder climbs gave me an affection for a creature worthy of Disney animation, a cute cardboard figure. My impression of a blacksnake was as unreal as the animated Bambi is from a real fawn.

And in my memory of the tiny, newly hatched bullsnake slithering through my fingers long ago, I also put aside the picture of that newborn snake—barely two minutes out of the egg—instinctively getting into striking position at the first opportunity.

If I had read anything other than what I wanted to read, or remembered anything other than what I wanted to remember, I would have been much more guarded in my next encounter with my charming pet snake Moon.

SIX

Moonstruck

Moon bit me on Friday.

I came out to the log house to write at about nine o'clock.

The log house is the perfect place for a writer—or for a blacksnake. The house is surrounded by woods—low dogwoods and sourwood, tall pines and oaks. There are sunlit clearings.

A small creek runs in front of the house. Ferns grow in the back. It is quiet except for the sounds of birds and frogs. A variety of colorful lizards—blue-tailed skinks and brown fence lizards—dart among the ferns. My favorites are the green anoles with the bright red throats that puff out on demand.

There is no television, no radio, no ringing phone. As I said, it's perfect.

When I started writing forty years ago, things were different. I lived with my husband and two (soon-to-be three) daughters in a small barracks apartment. I wrote on the kitchen table.

My typewriter stayed at my place at the table. I'd push it aside when we ate. Sometimes, if I was in the middle of fixing supper, I'd switch the typewriter to the counter so I could type as I cooked.

Here's an example of my kitchen-table writing. This appeared on the Post Scripts page of the July 29, 1961, issue of *The Saturday Evening Post*.

The Sense of Humor

"Son, did you hear the one about the bunny who was going to have his tonsils out and he asked the doctor not to give him Novocain, and the doctor said, 'Why not?', and the bunny said, 'Becauthe I'm the ether bunny'?"

"No, I didn't hear it, dad. How does it go?"

"That's the joke."

"I don't get it."

"Well, you see the joke is ether."

"I don't think ether's so funny."

"No, but see, it's just a pun on the word Easter— see, ether and Easter and . . ."

"Dear, did you hear the one about the bunny————"

"Yes, I heard you telling Billy."

"Bobby, did you hear the one about the bunny who was going to have his tonsils out and————"

"You mean the ether bunny?"

"Oh, James, did you hear the one about the bunny who couldn't take Novocain because he was the ether bunny?"

"Oh, that's a good one, boss. Ha ha ha, who who hee, that's really good. I'm going to have to—whoo

> whoo haa haa—remember that one. Who ho ho that
> is one of the ..."

BETSY BYARS

That wasn't great literature, but it does give you an idea of the two talents I started with:

1) An ease with words (which came from a lifelong habit of reading).

2) An ease with dialogue (which came from being born into a family of talkers).

Everything else I acquired the hard way—I learned it.

Back to the log house. When I arrived there on Friday, I saw Moon first thing. It was as if the snake were waiting for me.

It was at the back of the house, stretched out full-length on the wooden deck. Its eyes were open, but it appeared to be asleep. Snake's eyes are protected by a transparent cap, and this cap keeps their eyes open all the time. Maybe they are asleep, maybe not. Nobody knows.

I crossed the deck quietly and stood looking down at Moon. Moon's skin was a covering of overlapping scales. It was a uniform slatey black. It was clean, not slimy in the least, with a dull satiny finish. A blacksnake is a very handsome snake.

Moon did not move.

I know that snakes are shy. I know that snakes will try to get out of your way. I know that they will sometimes lie absolutely still, hoping (if snakes do hope) that they won't be seen. This was, for me, a large part of their attractiveness.

But Moon seemed more relaxed than shy, more laid back, contented even. Certainly there was nothing to indicate that the snake was nervous or concerned about my presence.

My dog, Harvey, had, as usual, come out to the log house with me. Harvey had paused to lift his leg on a few ferns. Then he started across the deck.

Harvey is a clumsy dog, and he makes about as much noise coming across a wooden deck as a clogger. Snakes are deaf to sound carried by air—I had read that—but Harvey makes a lot of vibrations, too, and snakes hear by sensing vibrations from the ground.

Moon's head rose. The large black eyes saw an unwelcome sight—a clumsy black dog.

With soundless grace, Moon slid halfway off the porch to the underside of the deck.

I say "halfway" because about forty inches of Moon still lay on the deck beside my feet. Moon was two-thirds under the deck, one-third on top.

Harvey advanced. I did not move except to reach over and open the sliding door for him so he could go in the house.

Harvey enjoys a good chase, but only with something that can be counted on to run in the opposite direction. Cats, lizards, and squirrels know the rules of a good sporting chase. Turtles don't. Turtles won't even try. And snakes are worse than turtles. Snakes get mad.

Harvey deals with this by pretending to be unable to see anything that won't play fair. So it did not surprise me at all that Harvey could not see Moon.

Head high, Harvey trotted past the forty inches of snake and went into the house.

The forty inches of snake at my feet did not move.

I slid the door shut and leaned over the railing to see what the rest of Moon was up to.

Moon was curved back, the head and eyes alert. The arch of its neck was braced against some water pipes on the side of the house. Its body formed an S.

I could see the bluish gray of the belly. Moon's head, in its doubled-back position, was close, but—I judged—not dangerously so.

Also, Moon didn't seem that uptight to me. Sure, the snake was alert. What snake wouldn't be with a Scotty dog clogging past it?

But, I figured, if the snake were really uptight, it wouldn't have left a good forty inches of itself stretched out on the deck where anybody who wanted to could—well, could grab it.

I had already started thinking along those lines. Well, not grabbing it exactly. But certainly this *was* my one chance to touch this snake, to know what it felt like.

And maybe I really would do a book about Moon. If so—my thoughts continued—I owed it to myself and to my readers to touch this snake and see what it felt like.

The first (and possibly the best) piece of writing advice I ever got was in third grade. "Write about what you know," Mrs. Stroupe told us.

At that time I went to a school in rural North Carolina, and I thought, Well, that is the stupidest thing I ever heard in my life. I mean, it may be fine to write about what you know if you're Lindbergh, but if you're a third grade girl in rural North Carolina, you better make up some stuff.

That's what I did. Through grade school, through high school, through college, even into my professional career, I made up stuff.

But at some point finally—finally!—I got smart. I saw *why* you write about what you know.

The words *author* and *authority* go hand in hand. If an author is writing about what she knows, she is writing with authority. It's as simple as that, and one of the best gifts a writer can give a reader is the feeling "This writer knows what she's talking about."

So in order to write with authority about this snake—see, I can talk myself into almost anything—I *had* to touch it.

The forty inches of tail were still there at my feet. It would be nice to touch the whole entire snake, of course, but forty inches was better than nothing.

I swallowed.

My mouth was dry.

I reached out and touched the tail. It was cool, dry, and smooth. The snake's skin crawled a little as if with revulsion at being touched.

I encircled the tail with my hand. My little finger was raised as politely as if I were reaching for a tea cup.

With the speed of lightning, the snake's head darted up over the side of the porch and caught my little finger. It was a move so stunning, so silent, that I felt no pain, just the sharp stab of panic.

I drew my hand back instinctively.

The head appeared again—another strike—this time mercifully, a miss.

I drew back so fast I lost my balance and fell down like a toddler. I scooted backward.

The head appeared one more time—one final attempt—but I was well out of reach now.

On these three strikes this snake had looked so fierce, so aggressive, that I would not have been surprised if it had come slithering across the deck after me. And that snake's mouth was *big*!

I sat with my arms crossed over my chest, waiting, praying.

I noticed now that the tail was gone. I hoped this meant the rest of the snake was gone, too. This was the first encouraging thing that had happened since I decided to become an authority on snakes.

Still I waited. I did not move. Stunned and shaken, I sat listening to my pounding heart.

The whole thing reminded me of a wooden toy I'd had as a child—a small wooden box. You slid the top back with your thumb and a little wooden snake sprang out, it's lone fang landing on your thumbnail.

I had never cared much for that little box.

After a moment I unwound my arms and looked at my finger. It was bleeding a lot.

I later learned that snake saliva apparently prevents coagulation of blood, and so a bite from a harmless snake bleeds profusely and looks more serious than it is.

I went into the house—heart still pounding—washed the cut, iodined it, and applied a Band-Aid.

Finally I went back to the deck. I leaned gingerly over the railing. I half-expected to see Moon lurking, still harboring a grudge, waiting for one final retaliation, but there was no sign of the snake.

I went down the steps and, kneeling, inspected the area under the deck. There were leaves and rocks, some bare earth—a crawl space of about six inches—but no Moon.

Either the snake could blend in with the leaves or could burrow beneath them or—the most likely possibility—was gone.

I watched for a while, letting my eyes adjust to the dim darkness. The only light filtered down through the boards, leaving a striped effect on the dry leaves.

Finally I gave up and went back into the log cabin.

I went down in the basement of the cabin where my husband was working.

"I thought you said blacksnakes are harmless," I said to my husband.

"They are."

"That is harmless?" I held up my little finger wrapped in a Band-Aid.

"You must have tormented the snake."

"Torment? Me? I know better than to torment a snake!"

"Well, what were you doing?"

"Nothing. I wasn't doing anything!"

"Then it wouldn't have bitten you."

"I touched . . . touched its tail, and the worst part is that I can hardly remember what it felt like! I got this for nothing!"

I had now known Moon for three days. In the course of those three days I had experienced fascination, admiration, affection, fear, pain, and—the most important thing in any relationship—respect.

SEVEN

The Write Stuff

Here's the way I personally rate the elements of a story in importance:

Characters

Plot

Setting

Good Scraps

(And most of the other things—like theme and mood—I don't think about.)

The plot of a book usually comes first. It's a seed, one idea, and what I'm looking for in this idea is something with possibilities—like kids swimming at night in someone's pool, like a character lost in the woods, like kids in a foster home.

But even though the plot comes first, it is not the most important thing. The characters are the key to the story. They unlock the plot. They make it happen. So the characters, for me, are the most important element.

The setting varies in importance. Sometimes it's very important, as in *The House of Wings,* and I spend a lot of time making the setting real to the reader. At other times the setting is not important at all, and so I use a generic setting, as in *Pinballs.*

Plenty of good scraps are as important in making a book as in the making of a quilt.

I often think of my books as scrapbooks of my life, because I put in them all the neat things that I see and read and hear. I sometimes wonder what people who don't write do with all their good stuff.

Here are some of the neat things I have put in my books:

- A blacksnake on my front porch.
- Ninety-year-old twins who were still dressing alike.
- A man who could smell snakes. (He said they had a musty, sweet smell like old brown bread, but Moon doesn't have any smell at all.)
- A woman who made varmint stew from dead things she found on the road.
- A dog named Mud.
- A cat with a golden earring.
- An extra hippopotamus.
- An owl in the bathroom.
- Puce tennis shoes.
- A gift-wrapped dime.

I'll pause to tell you where I got the scrap about the gift-wrapped dime.

I was six years old. We were living in the country, near the cotton mill where my father worked. It was my sister's birthday, and my mother was throwing a party for her.

Now, this was during the Depression and people were poor. When kids were invited to a party, they didn't rush downtown and buy an electronic game. They looked around the house until they spotted something that nobody wanted any more, and they wrapped it up and off the kid went to the party.

My sister got an unusual assortment of gifts that year. I, who loved unusual things, was green with envy. She got a pair of celluloid cuffs that office workers used to put on their arms to keep their blouse cuffs clean. I loved the celluloid cuffs and borrowed them at every opportunity.

There was one tiny gift wrapped in notebook paper. I must have been an unimaginative child because I kept saying, "Open the little one! Open the little one!"

I thought it was probably a ring, but anybody who could afford to give my sister a ring could afford a piece of real wrapping paper, so what could it be?

At last she opened it. It was a dime.

And that gift-wrapped dime stayed in my mind for the rest of my life, even after I gave it to Harold V. Coleman in the gift exchange in *After the Goat Man*.

More scraps:

• A boy who did imitations of whales.

• Garbage Dog. (He got his name because he sat out by the school cafeteria door and everyone threw their leftovers into his mouth.)

• A cherry twig toothbrush.

• A dog with a turtle in his mouth.

I'll tell you about that one, too.

When my daughter was about six, she had a small turtle, the kind you used to be able to buy in Woolworth's for fifty cents.

She cleaned the bowl and put the bowl and the turtle on the porch to get some sun. She went out an hour later and the turtle was gone.

This was a real mystery. The turtle could not possibly have

crawled out of the bowl, and every member of the family swore they hadn't hidden it for a joke.

Then we noticed that Rudy, a red dog from down the street, was sitting at the edge of the steps. Rudy looked worried, and we noticed that he wasn't closing his mouth all the way. My daughter went over, forced Rudy's mouth open, and out plopped the turtle, good as new.

What had happened, we figured, was that Rudy had come along, seen this nice bowl of clean water, bent down to drink, and ended up with a turtle in his mouth.

I thought a lot about Rudy sitting there, really very dignified, with a turtle in his mouth. I just loved it.

So in *The 18th Emergency,* Garbage Dog comes strolling up and Ezzie notices the dog's mouth isn't closed all the way. He checks it out and there's the turtle.

Now this is my last scrap. It's the worst and the hardest to tell.

• A dead man whose mouth popped open.

I was five when this happened. I was visiting my grandparents. My grandfather kept a country store, and I was over there one morning making my selection at the candy counter when my grandfather asked me if I'd like to go with him to pay his respects to Uncle Joe.

I said, "Sure."

We got in his truck and drove a long way into the country. We got out of the truck and went into a house filled with people. We went into the living room. There was a home-built wooden coffin in the center of the room. I didn't know what a coffin was. I had never seen a dead person.

My grandfather led me over and picked me up so that I could see inside the coffin.

As he picked me up, my leg kicked out, jarring the coffin, and

Uncle Joe's mouth popped open. His mouth was stuffed with rags.

I don't remember anything beyond that one horrifying moment, but for a long, long time I didn't want to die because I was afraid of having rags in my mouth. My mother explained that the rags supported the chin and kept it from crumpling but I still didn't like it.

When I was writing *The Pinballs,* it was Mr. Mason whose leg kicked out, jarring the coffin, and who saw Uncle Joe's mouth pop open.

Mr. Mason ran all the way home and hid under the bed, which is probably what I felt like doing. But I'm sure I got back in the truck with my grandfather and drove back to the store.

So my formula for a good book is:
- A plot with possibilities.
- Characters to make the plot happen.
- A believable setting.
- Lots and lots of good scraps.

EIGHT

Moon in My Hands

"Snake! Snake! There it is!"

I was leaning against the porch railing, drinking a cup of coffee, when I glanced down and saw Moon below on the ground.

"There it is!" I was enormously excited because I had not seen Moon in three weeks.

Ed had come out to the log house that morning and joined me on the porch. "So?"

I don't know why seeing this particular snake caused me such pleasure and excitement, except to say I was like Tom, a character in *The Midnight Fox*. He says, "I cannot exactly explain my fascination with this fox. It was as if I had just learned a new and exciting game that I wanted to play more than anything else in the world. . . . The rules I didn't exactly know yet: all I had so far was a fierce desire to play."

Moon was a new game to me.

Below, on the ground, Moon was making its way in slow, relaxed S-curves toward the woods.

"I'm going to follow and see where it goes."

I went down the steps and around the side of the house. Moon sensed my presence and began to pick up speed.

I picked up speed, too.

My husband was still on the porch, and from that vantage point he called out directions. "No, more to the right! It's going down the hill—no, now it's going toward the pines!"

Finally we both lost sight of the snake.

Ed came down and we looked through the brush. "I know it didn't get as far as the clearing," Ed said. "I'd have seen that. It's got to be in this area . . . somewhere."

"Unless it went underground."

"There!" My husband pointed directly at my feet.

I looked down.

"I still don't—*YIIIIIIII!*"

I don't know why I screamed. It's just what you do when you look down and see a big snake right by your shoe.

Fortunately snakes can't hear even high-pitched screams, and Moon didn't move.

"I stepped right over it!" I said. "I could have stepped on it!"

Although Moon was a uniform slatey black in color, it could take on a sticklike appearance by sort of zigzagging the body. Ed and I stood watching Moon, and it did not seem to mind being watched.

This snake really seemed like a work of art to me. It could move agilely without legs. It could eat food bigger than its head. It had this nice clean rainproof skin. It took care of itself. It shed its skin. It never made a sound. Plus it was beautiful and mysterious and commanded respect.

I kept watching.

I had—for the past weeks—been reading a lot of snake

books. I had found myself reading with special interest the chapters dealing with snake capture.

Of course I had no intention of capturing Moon and putting him in a snake cage—even though the directions for making such a cage were also included and didn't look that hard.

One of the reasons I didn't want Moon in a cage was because the instructions for force-feeding a snake that refuses food—and blacksnakes were listed among those that "commonly refuse to eat"—did look hard. The thought of force-feeding a snake really turned me off.

Here are two ways to force-feed a snake (so you can see why I didn't want to do it):

· You hold the snake firmly behind the head, force its mouth open, and gently but firmly force a young mouse down its throat. If the snake refuses to swallow, you massage the lump of mouse gently until it does go down.

· You buy some pill capsules from the drugstore and fill them with chopped mouse (which, incidentally, you cannot buy in any grocery store—you've got to make your own chopped mouse) and force one down the reluctant snake's throat.

All I wanted to do was capture it long enough to hold it and see what it felt like. I had read in the book that snakes felt cool and dry, but I wanted to see this for myself. I wanted to know how much it weighed, how heavy it was.

And I might write about it.

The fact that "I might write about it" had talked me into a lot of things in my life. Like:

· Going on Space Mountain at Disney World.
· Taking flying lessons.
· Learning to play Galaxians.
· Flying across the U.S. in a 1940 J-3 Cub that only holds twelve gallons of gas.
· Learning to use a computer.

Incidentally, some things I did not talk myself into doing (but wrote about anyway) were:

- Going over rapids in a homemade raft.
- Getting bitten by a rattlesnake.
- Breaking into city jail.
- Flying off a roof with cloth wings.
- Swimming in a neighbor's pool in my underwear.
- Spending the night in a garbage dumpster.
- Crossing the ice on a frozen river, falling through the thin ice, and drowning.

I was already sure that I was going to talk myself into writing about picking up Moon, so I made a forked stick according to the directions in a *Boy's Guide to Snakes*. The guide had suggested that many boys would prefer to collect their subjects bare-handed, but I had a pair of gloves alongside my forked stick—just in case.

But my forked stick was back at the house, and I was fairly sure Moon wasn't going to wait for me to run and get it.

Moon was still relaxed. There was a slight bulge a few inches back from his head—possibly a frog. This would make capture easier since I could put my forked stick—if I'd had it—between the bulge and the head.

I told Ed, "I wish I had my forked stick."

"Why?"

"So I could catch it. I want to see what it feels like."

"Put your foot on its head—very gently—and then pick it up behind it."

"You've got to be kidding."

"You want me to pick it up for you?"

"No, I want to do it myself."

"You want me to hold the head down with a stick?"

"Please."

Ed got a stick. Moon was still there, coiled in what was a striking position, but it didn't appear to be ready to strike.

"Here goes."

Ed lowered the stick onto Moon's neck.

Instantly Moon came to life. It was as if Ed were delivering a bolt of electricity through the stick. The whole body was writhing.

"Oh . . . oh."

"Pick it up!"

"I can't. It's moving too fast."

"Pick it up!"

"That's what I'm trying to do!"

I bent.

I picked up the snake.

Immediately the snake wrapped itself around my arm. I had the head. The body had me.

"Ed, Ed, look what it's doing. Why is it doing this? Ed, help me!"

"Are you through holding it?"

"Yes! Yes!"

"Then just put it down."

"I can't! It won't let go of me!"

"If you let go of it, it'll let go of you."

"How do you know?"

"I know."

Actually Moon and I let go at about the same time. I jumped back, and Moon dropped to the ground and took off.

One of a blacksnake's popular names is black racer, and the snake lived up to the name now. It took off like an arrow.

I read in one of the snake books that the fastest speed a blacksnake had been clocked at was about 3.7 miles an hour. But it sure looked a lot faster than that to me.

When my heart had stopped pounding, I said, "Next time when I pick it up—"

"There's going to be a next time?"

"Yes, of course. I read in one of my snake books that repeated handlings make a snake more docile."

"I see."

To be honest, I did not see how handlings such as Moon had just survived could make a snake docile, but it sounded good.

"Next time I'm going to try and hold the head in one hand and the tail in the other. That way it won't be able to wrap around my arm. It's really distracting to have a snake around your arm. It makes it almost impossible to concentrate on what it feels like!"

This is a picture of my parents, Nan Rugheimer and Guy Cromer, taken on a beach near Charleston, S.C., during their courtship.

My first formal portrait to celebrate the fact that I was one year old. This is the only time I was a cute kid. It was all downhill from here.

(right) My sister Nancy, my mother, and I. Nancy and I wore our hair like this until we were in junior high. I am the one in the tam. Nancy is the one with the new watch.

(below right) I was about seven. The rabbit was named Danny.

(below left) My father is holding Billy, and I'm holding Buttsy. Buttsy used to push me in the hammock.

The summer of 1942. I was fourteen. My father and I are in the galley of his boat the Nan-a-Bet.

I was a senior in high school when this was taken. Nancy was in college, a math major. I was going to major in math, too. Sister mathematicians.

Urbana, Illinois, 1956. Behind us are the barracks where I began to write. I really had two choices—write or lose my mind. I wrote.

My four children (l. to r.): Nan, Betsy, Guy, and Laurie. Guy did the computer graphics for The Computer Nut *and two of my daughters are now writing books of their own.*

Moon and I. It's hard to tell who is the most uncomfortable.

I only got part of Moon in this picture. He seems to go on forever. He's a very long snake.

This is not a picture of two Freckles. It's Freckles and his reflection in the plexiglass side of his cage.

This is Satellite, coming out from between the railroad ties—a favorite place.

Here I am running the wing of my husband's sailplane. The sailplane is hooked to an airplane by a long tow rope, and I hold the wings level until they get going.

Me and my Yellow Bird. I got my pilot's license in this plane on December 19, 1984.

Ed and I and the J-3 Piper Cub upon our arrival at the San Luis Obispo Airport.

That Lucky Old Moon

One Friday in August I was driving out to the log house, and I saw a dead blacksnake in the middle of the road. It had recently been run over by a car, but not more than once or twice. For a dead snake it was in pretty good shape.

The snake was about the same size as Moon and about the same color. I slowed down, stopped, and rolled down the window.

The snake did look like Moon, but I had reason to think it wasn't. According to the snake books I'd read:

• Moon wouldn't start traveling to the place of hibernation until October. This was just the first of August.

• Blacksnakes usually do not leave their summer feeding ground, and Moon had not even begun to make a dent in the frogs and lizards around the log house.

• Plus, there were baby lizards hatching daily in the lily bed, and Moon could slither through the lilies, eating these like popcorn.

But the main reason I did not think it was Moon was because I did not want it to be Moon. This dead blacksnake was somebody else's blacksnake, an unlucky one.

I started driving again and turned into the shaded, twisting road to the log house. I began driving slower as my brain began to perk.

If I went back and picked up the dead snake, I thought, I would have a chance to look at it up real close, something I was obviously not going to be able to do with a live snake like Moon.

I could see the scales and the teeth. I could examine the way the scales are different on the underside, enabling the snake to slither. I could feel the weight.

Actually, my thoughts continued, it was lucky that I saw the snake. This was a wonderful once-in-a-lifetime opportunity. Plus, I had a paper bag on the floor of the backseat to put it in.

This was meant to be.

I did a U-turn and started back down the road, heading for the blacksnake.

Luck has played a big, big part in my writing. Many of my books grew out of simply being at the right place at the right time. Like:

• I was driving home from town one afternoon when we were living in West Virginia, and I happened to hear a news bulletin about an old man known as the Goat Man who had boarded himself up in his cabin (with a loaded shotgun) to keep the highway from going through his house. That news bulletin grew into *After the Goat Man*.

• I was walking in the woods near our cabin in West Virginia one afternoon, and I came upon a fox. It wasn't a black fox, but it was a stunning moment for me. I just stopped cold. I looked at that fox and the fox looked at me for what seemed like an eternity—though it couldn't have been because I held my breath the whole time. Then with a leap that seemed lighter than air, the fox was gone. That incident grew into *The Midnight Fox.*

• I read a story in the newspaper one night about a huge flying creature that had flown into someone's TV antenna. The next night a man was going into his barn and the "huge flying creature" came flying out at him. The newspaper started calling it the Morgantown Monster, and it was big local news. Well, the Morgantown Monster turned out to be a sandhill crane, lost and injured in migration. That story grew into *The House of Wings.*

• I looked up one day from a manuscript I was working on, and there on a porch beam happened to be a snake. This was a snake that, as far as I know, has never been up on that beam before or since.

Those things are luck.

Now maybe I would have heard something else and seen something else, and I would have gone on to write other books in place of those. But I know I wouldn't have written *After the Goat Man, The Midnight Fox,* and *The House of Wings.* And I never would have started *The Moon and I.*

So seeing the dead blacksnake was—to my way of thinking—a lucky break.

I drove to the place where the snake lay and pulled off onto the berm of the road. I sat in the car while some traffic went by—fortunately on the other side of the road.

I didn't want to jump out and pick up the snake while cars were driving past. Motorists seeing me do that might think I was a crazy lady instead of a sensible, intelligent author.

(Also, in one of my books I had a character named Mad Mary, who ate dead creatures off the road, and I didn't want anyone to think that character was based on myself and that I was picking up supper.)

Finally there was a lull in the traffic. I leaped out of the car with my paper sack. I picked up the snake by the tail. It was stuck to the road where it had been run over, but I swallowed my uneasiness, pulled hard, stuffed the snake in the paper bag, and threw the bag on the floor of the backseat.

I whipped into the driver's seat and closed the door. I had not been observed.

I U-turned and started for the log house, where I could examine my snake in private.

I began to whistle. I felt exhilarated, almost lightheaded, as if I had done something dangerous and exciting, as if I had pulled off some special caper, some feat. This was *National Enquirer* headline stuff—

WOMAN CAPTURES DEAD SNAKE WHISTLING DIXIE

I drove on, congratulating myself with every rotation of the tires. I was coming to a busy intersection so I put on my turn blinker, pulled into the turn lane, and waited. I could not possibly have been more pleased with myself.

Then I heard a noise.

Crin . . . kle.

I stopped being pleased with myself and my light-headedness turned to fear.

Crin . . . (I waited. My heart had stopped beating.) *. . . kle.*

To make my heart start up again, I told myself, Listen, paper bags unfold all the time, even empty ones, even ones that don't have snakes in them. Perfectly normal paper bags crinkle.

I turned down the radio so I could keep track of the crinkles.

When I was a kid, I could watch *the* scariest movie in the world—as long as I could put my fingers in my ears. Today, I can watch *the* scariest movie on TV—as long as I can turn the volume off.

Like in *The Mummy*. That was *the* scariest movie I saw as a kid. Well, every time the mummy was coming, the frogs would stop croaking. There would be a silence. And that silence was so scary I'd have to put my fingers in my ears to block it out.

After the silence would come something worse—the sound of the mummy approaching. *Sliiiiiide* . . . step . . . *sliiiiiide* . . . step. (The mummy limped.)

Of course I never heard the *sliiiiiide* . . . steps because my fingers were in my ears.

If I could have put my fingers in my ears now, I would have. I couldn't, though, because I was gripping the steering wheel with them.

In the silence it came again.

Crin . . . *kle. Crin* . . .

While I was waiting for the . . . *kle,* the man in the car behind me blew his horn.

I looked up, ready to drive forward, but an eighteen wheeler had come into view. I waited.

Even the sound of an eighteen wheeler couldn't drown out that . . . *kle* when it finally came.

Plus, this . . . *kle* had a different, louder sound, as if the bag was now open.

I knew that if that snake had managed to slip out of the bag, and if that snake managed to slip under the seat, and if that snake managed to touch my ankle, I would press down on the gas and shoot forward directly into the path of the eighteen wheeler or anything else that was unfortunate enough to get in my way.

The truck passed, and the man behind me sounded his horn again. This time, heart firmly in my throat, I did drive forward.

At the first available opportunity I did something intelligent.

I pulled off the road, threw the gear shift into park, jumped out of the car, and slammed the door behind me.

TEN

Hep

"Can I hep you?" a voice said.

I turned.

A man in a pickup truck had stopped in the road. He asked the question out of the window.

I had been standing beside the car, looking through the window at the paper bag (which to my relief still appeared to be closed), wondering how all this had happened, when the truck arrived.

I tried to look unconcerned because I didn't want the truck driver to catch on to the fact that I was scared of a paper bag.

"Car givin' you trouble?"

"Oh, no, my car's fine," I said with forced cheer. "My car couldn't be better."

The man did not seem convinced. He continued to look at me like I was something out of left field. It didn't take but about thirty seconds for me to blurt out the truth.

As always, I told too much. (This has been one of the hardest, most unnatural things about my writing—to keep myself from telling too much. It's my nature to overdo everything.)

Somehow the man managed to keep a straight face while he listened.

"See, I stopped my car because I picked up this snake? And I put it in a paper bag? And I thought the snake was dead? And then I heard the bag going *crin-kle, crin-kle,* like that, and I was afraid the snake wasn't dead? I was afraid that it was going to come out of the bag and crawl under the seat and touch me on the ankle."

The man still kept a straight face.

"And this," I finished to his relief and my own, "would cause me to have a wreck."

I stopped short of mentioning that I was afraid the wreck would make the local newspaper and the headline would be—

AUTHOR THINKS DEAD SNAKE TOUCHES ANKLE
AND CAUSES TEN VEHICLE PILEUP.

"Want some hep?"

"Oh, yes, please."

The man parked the pickup truck behind my car. "You better step out of the road, ma'am."

I walked out of the road, around the car, and stood behind him while he opened the door of the car.

We peered in together.

The paper bag wasn't moving. Paper bags never move when you want them to—it's like the mole creatures in the back of my closet when I was little. Still, the man hesitated.

"What kind of snake was it you picked up?"

"Blacksnake."

He seemed not to trust my identification, so I added, "But it was dead. You probably think I'm making this up—but it really was dead and then it moved."

"I believe you, ma'am. A dead snake can bite a person same as a live one."

"Are you kidding me?"

"No, ma'am, a buddy of mine killed a rattler—chopped its head off with a hoe, and when he picked it up, the head bit him."

"The *head* bit him?"

"That's right, ma'am—caught him right there." The man pinched the flesh between his thumb and forefinger. "It's a reflex action they have."

While I watched, the man took out the paper bag and dropped it on the ground. It didn't move. He opened it, looked inside, and upended the bag.

The dead snake slid out and landed at our feet. It was a sorry sight. It wasn't moving now and looked even deader than it had when I picked it up off the road.

The man prodded it with his foot. "It might have moved," he said, "but it sure ain't going to move anymore."

I nodded.

"Anyway, it's not a blacksnake, it's a rat snake."

"How do you know?"

"The color is different, and the scales are coarser."

"I have a blacksnake at my house," I said, "and it looked the same to me. You must know a lot about snakes."

"Some."

"What do they like to eat?" I had been thinking of providing some treats for Moon—something up close to the house that I could keep tabs on. I couldn't keep tabs on the frogs and lizards.

"Eggs."

"Bird eggs." I had read that in one of the snake books.

"Hen eggs, too."

"Hen eggs?"

"Yes, ma'am."

"How could a snake swallow such a thing?"

"They stretch out their jaws and kind of press down on the egg. It's a sight all right. After they get the egg past their throat, they kind of kink their backbone and break it."

"My."

"I've heard of snakes going in a hen house and eating a glass egg that was put in a nest to make the hens lay."

"My, my."

There was a pause. I felt as if I'd just swallowed something undigestable myself.

"You still want this snake, ma'am?"

"Oh, no, just let it go."

He gave me another of his straight-faced looks. With his foot he nudged the dead snake into the ditch.

I picked up the bag and put it in the back of the car.

"Listen, thank you so much for stopping," I said. "I just wanted to see that snake up real close. This all probably seemed awfully stupid to you."

"No ma'am," he said galantly.

He touched his hand to his baseball cap as he made his way to his truck.

"Glad to be of hep," he added.

ELEVEN

The First Skateboard
in the History of the World

You already know the things I was scared of when I was little, but I'll refresh your memory.

- mummies
- Bubba
- Noises
- Getting dead and having rags stuffed in my mouth
- The molelike creatures that lived in the back of my closet and hid everytime my mother opened the door

Here are the things I wasn't afraid of:

- Snakes
- Animals
- Hurricanes
- Tornadoes
- Deep water
- White water
- And anything else you could name.

Since none of my friends knew I was scared of anything, I was thought to be a tough little kid.

My bravery (and the rest of me) was about seven years old when I was selected by the neighborhood to test ride The First Skateboard in the History of the World.

I didn't even know what a skateboard was. This was the summer of 1935. Skateboards hadn't been invented back then. But that did not stop our neighborhood from making one.

Here's what went into The First Skateboard in the History of the World:

One board.

Forty-two assorted nails.

One roller skate.

Back then, roller skates were made out of metal and could be adjusted to stretch waaaay out for long feet, which a lot of us had. We stretched this skate out so far that it came apart. This suited us just fine. We nailed the front half of the skate to the front of the board and the back half to the back.

Then we turned the board over and hammered the tips of the nails (which had come through the board) down—hard. We had a deep respect for nails. We had all stepped on nails at one time or another, and even though we protested all the way to the doctor's office, "It wasn't rusty! I swear it wasn't rusty! If you don't believe me ask Skrunky! He'll tell you it wasn't rusty!" we still got a shot. We also had a deep respect for shots.

The whole construction took less than five minutes, and the skateboard was ready to go. By this time we knew it was a skateboard because the leader of the neighborhood—a sixth grade girl named Bee—said, "Who wants to go first on the skateboard?"

There was a silence.

Then Bee answered her own question. "Betsy will."

There was a sort of echo from the rest, "Betsy will-ill-ill-ill-ill."

And that was how I—seven-year-old Betsy Alice Cromer—

got the honor of testing The First Skateboard in the History of the World.

At the time it didn't seem like an honor, more like a military duty.

However, we always did what Bee told us to do. The explanation "Bee told me to" often made my mother explode with, "And if Bee told you to stick your head in a lion's mouth, would you?" "If Bee told you to jump off the Empire State Building, would you?" Well . . . I was glad it never came to those things.

We took the skateboard to the top of Magnolia Avenue, which was the street I lived on. Magnolia Avenue was not a steep hill, but the sidewalk had been buckled by the roots of old trees, and it was considered challenging for a skater.

We put the skateboard down on the sidewalk.

Bee said, "Go ahead, Betsy."

I said, "I will."

Fortunately we were unfamiliar with skateboards, and we didn't know you were supposed to stand up on them, so I sat down. Otherwise I wouldn't be alive today.

I sat, put my feet up on the skateboard, and held on to the sides with both hands.

Somebody gave me a push.

I rolled a few inches but came to a stop at the first wide crack in the sidewalk.

They pushed again—harder.

Same disappointing ride.

"This hill isn't steep enough," Bee complained, "I vote we take it to Red Hill."

"Red Hill-ill-ill-ill," came the echo.

The echo had a scary ring to it this time because Red Hill was the Alps, the Himalayas, and Mount Everest all rolled into one.

We weren't allowed to roller-skate down Red Hill. We

weren't even allowed to ride our bikes down it. But nobody had told us we couldn't *skateboard* down it.

We set off in a silence tense with excitement. My throat was dry. I had recently recovered from a broken arm—the result of a daring feat on the monkey bars in Dilworth Park.

See, we had been having a contest to see who could hang on to the bars by one hand the longest, and I held on so long that my body began to angle out to the side, as if I were doing a gymnastic display of agility, which I wasn't. When I finally let go, I was horizontal to the ground and landed on my left elbow, which showed its displeasure by snapping in two. (I did win the contest, but neither of my parents congratulated me on the win.)

By the time we reached the top of Red Hill, my left arm was throbbing a warning like jungle drums.

And we reached the top of Red Hill very quickly.

"Sit down," Bee said.

I didn't want to, but I had to. Bee had told me to. I sat down on the skateboard. I said, "Now don't push me till I'm ready and I'm not ready yet so don't push me till I say I'm ready, till I say 'Go.' Then when I say 'Go,' I only want Wilma to push me"—Wilma was the weak link in the gang—"and until I say 'Go,' everybody stay back and leave me—"

The neighborhood gang heard only the "Go" and they pushed. And I went.

The first thing that happened was that all the skin was scraped off my knuckles. (I was holding onto the sides of the board and my weight in the center of the board brought it closer to the road than anticipated.)

The next thing that happened was a three-part miracle.

The skate broke off the back of the board, the back of the board acted as a brake, and The First Skateboard in the History of the World ground to a halt twenty feet down Red Hill.

There were cries of disappointment and of determination to renail the skate and start all over again, but these cries were drowned out by my own.

"I knew it wasn't going to work! Look what it did to my fingers! If you don't know how to make skateboards, don't make skateboards! Anyway, there is no such thing as a skateboard and there never will be!"

I stormed down the hill. My shouts of outrage turned to whimpers of pain as I got out of the gang's earshot and saw the damage to my knuckles. I grew silent as I got within earshot of 915 Magnolia Avenue, my home. I liked to administer my own first-aid treatments because I was the only one who would stop administering if it hurt.

"What have you done now?" my mother asked, seeing me at the bloodied basin.

I gave my usual answer. "Nothing."

"What—have—you—done—now?" My mother always added the word *now* to give the impression that I did a lot of things.

"I went down Red Hill on a skateboard."

"A what?"

"A board with a skate on the bottom."

"I suppose Bee told you to."

Silence.

"And if Bee told you to catch a train to Timbuktu, would you?"

Probably.

So the test ride of the skateboard came and went without notice, without acclaim. I never got on another one. I never will.

But when I see kids on skateboards doing 180 ollies, ollie impossibles, lipslides, and G-turns, I think to myself, You guys would never believe it to look at me now, but I actually test rode The First Skateboard in the History of the World.

TWELVE

What to Do When You Can't Find Your Blacksnake (Or Start Your Next Chapter)

There is no easy way to find a blacksnake that doesn't want to be found. Blacksnakes are secretive, timid, and cautious. I accept that.

Blacksnakes hide when they are digesting food. Their prey is sometimes large and is always swallowed whole. I accept that.

Digestion—which even dissolves the victim's bones—may take a week or more. I accept that, too. Bones are definitely hard to digest.

But come on now, it couldn't take more than a few days to digest a measly lizard or frog.

So where was Moon? I had not seen the snake for over a month, and I had been actively looking for it—putting on boots and wading the length of the creek, trooping through the woods, checking every place I had ever seen it or any place that blacksnakes were known to like.

Summer is a lazy time for snakes—they mostly just hang out—but where?

I really missed Moon!

As the Moon-less days passed, I kept telling myself that Moon was probably somewhere digesting, and I kept reminding myself that all the books said that snakes don't wander, that they pretty much stay in one place until it's time to hibernate, that just because you don't see a snake doesn't mean that it doesn't see you.

And most of all, I kept telling myself that with blacksnakes, like everything in nature, a person must sometimes resort to waiting patiently.

The trouble is that waiting patiently is one of the things I am terrible at. I will do anything to keep from waiting patiently. When I first began to write, it was the thing I really, really hated. Like:

I would get one idea for a book, and I would write the book, and I would send it off. There would be rewrites and revisions and galley proof sheets to go over, but finally everything would be done, and then the only thing for me to do was to wait for the next idea.

Sometimes this waiting would go on for months. I would sit around, marking time, waiting like a tick for a dog to come by.

I would get more and more desperate because I always felt that now—now!—I had finally learned something about writing. Now—now!—I was ready to put all this self-taught, hard-earned knowledge into practice. Now I was equipped to write the best book in the entire world.

The only thing that was stopping me was that I didn't have an idea.

Finally, usually just when I had given up all hope, the idea would come, and I would be off—not, of course, writing the best book in the world but the best book I was capable of writing.

As I became more experienced, I learned that I don't need the perfect idea, with all the details in place, I just need an idea with possibilities, something that will allow my imagination to go to work. I now have more ideas than I can ever use. Indeed, I sometimes work on two manuscripts at once.

Also, I have over the years developed ways to avoid even the smallest of waits.

• When I finish one chapter in a manuscript and can't think of a way to start the next one.

I don't just sit around and wait for an idea to come to me. I go after it. I'm sort of like a reporter after a news item.

The first thing I do is go to the library. Then I walk along the shelves, pulling down book after book. I read the first sentence in every chapter.

Nothing.

I keep going. More books. More first lines.

Nothing.

Finally I will come to a chapter that starts with a sentence like "The phone rang."

I will snap the book shut. That's it! The phone is going to ring and it's going to be so-and-so, and so-and-so is going to tell what's-his-name that . . .

Before long I'm back in front of my word processor typing away.

• When I come to a serious stopping place in a book and can't go on.

This is usually when I, the author, have no idea what's going to happen. I can't even imagine what could happen. I'm stumped.

Once again, I don't just sit there and wait for a solution to come to me.

I sit down with my manuscript. I separate myself (mentally) from being the author of the book. I become the reader of the book.

I start reading.

What I'm looking for is this: What does the reader think is going to happen? What have I led the reader to expect will happen?

For example, I may have spent two hundred words describing a tree just because I felt like describing a tree. But what I was saying to the reader was watch out for this tree! This tree is important! I wouldn't have you read two hundred words about a tree if that tree wasn't going to fall on somebody or somebody wasn't going to fall out of it.

• When I come to a fork in the road.

This doesn't happen often, but I occasionally do come to a place where I can see two completely different ways the story can go. And the result will be two completely different books.

This happened in *Cracker Jackson* when Alma and her baby, Nicole, were in the hospital. Alma was going to be all right, but Nicole was in a coma, and I couldn't decide whether Nicole would live or die.

The book would be more powerful if Nicole died—and most writers want a powerful book—but I didn't want Nicole to die.

So I stopped. And I waited.

The answer came unexpectedly. I was giving a talk at a conference, and I was sitting with another author, waiting for the meeting to begin.

Some kids came up to talk to us while we were waiting, and I could hardly concentrate on my conversation because I was listening to hers. She was saying, "I couldn't help it! I just couldn't help it!"

After the kids were gone, I turned to the other author and said, "What was that all about?"

She said, "In one of my books I had a baby that the reader came to care about, and the baby died. Kids ask me why I 'made' the baby die. I tell them I couldn't help it, but they won't accept that."

I thought to myself, Maybe *you* couldn't help it, but I think I can, and when I got home, I went back to my word processor and in the very next chapter Nicole opened her eyes.

The answers always come if I wait, but it still isn't easy for me.

I tried to wait patiently for Moon to reappear, but I couldn't stop thinking about it.

"I haven't seen Moon in ages," I said to my husband a few days later. "I'm afraid the snake has moved on. All the snake books say it's around here somewhere, but I can't find it!"

"I just—" my husband began, but I was too upset to let him finish.

"I'm afraid I turned it off by picking it up. I know it didn't like it or it wouldn't have thrashed around so much. I'm afraid it's never coming back."

"I just drove around it. It's in the middle of the driveway."

"Moon?"

"Yes."

"Where?"

"Just walk down the driveway. You can't miss it."

I ran out of the house and down the drive. There Moon was—in the middle of the driveway doing a fabulous impersonation of a stick.

It had rained that morning after a three-week drought, and Moon had apparently come out to lie on the warm, wet tarmac.

A faint mist rose from the drive, giving the snake an element of mystery.

One surprising thing about Moon was that the snake did not mind being looked at. As long as I stood still, it was as if I were a tree. Either the snake didn't mind or it was asleep.

I leaned against a tree and just enjoyed the moment. I knew now that they were going to be rare.

Ten minutes passed . . . fifteen . . .

The snake lifted its head. It went into motion. Its body, at rest, had had a thick, heavy look, but as it began to move the body stretched out.

I followed slowly.

The snake continued, picking up a little speed, increasing the distance between us.

It slid off the road and into a hole beside an old tree stump. In a matter of seconds Moon was gone.

THIRTEEN

Miss Harriet's Room

When I was four, my mother took my sister downtown, and this is what my mother and Nancy came home with:

- A plaid book satchel
- A box of brand-new crayons
- Assorted dark plaid dresses, new brown shoes, new socks, new sweater
- A pencil box with little drawers that opened, and in the drawers were a ruler and a two-sided eraser and pencils and a pencil sharpener and a compass and a lot of other things I didn't know the names of.

My sister was going to school.

Up until this moment I had never had the faintest desire to go to school. I was perfectly content to run wild. Back then there were no preschools or kindergartens, so children generally ran wild until the age of six.

I would have been perfectly content to run wild for the rest of my life if I had not seen the pencil box. I wanted that pencil box. I coveted that pencil box. That pencil box was a symbol of everything that I wanted and was going to have to wait three years to get! Back then, three years was an eternity.

My sister went to school and her teacher's name was Miss Harriet, and my envy of the pencil box was nothing compared to my envy of what went on in Miss Harriet's room.

The kids painted in Miss Harriet's room—and not just pictures. They painted orange crates and furniture, and they had to have one of their father's old shirts to do this painting in. No one in my family had ever been allowed to have one of my father's old shirts—they were sacred—but my sister got one for Miss Harriet's room.

The kids made a store in Miss Harriet's room, and they had to bring little empty boxes to stock the store and purses so that they could go shopping at the store. No one in my family had been allowed to have one of my mother's old purses—they, too, were sacred—but my sister got one for Miss Harriet's room.

Miss Harriet read the kids a book called *The Adventures of Mabel,* and it was the best book in the world—my sister described it to me, chapter by chapter, and I looked forward to hearing Miss Harriet read it the way other kids looked forward to the circus.

Well, the three years finally passed, and I was ready for first grade. At last I would have Miss Harriet and make the store and the terrarium—yes, they made one of those, too—and hear *The Adventures of Mabel.* Now I would begin to *live!*

I was herded into the auditorium with the other new students and the principal introduced the teachers, who stood and smiled. We were cautioned to listen very carefully for our names so we could follow our teachers to our rooms.

You could have heard a pin drop.

Mrs. Clark's class was called. Mrs. Clark's class filed out of the auditorium.

Then came Miss Harriet. There was a flurry of anticipation because everyone, it turned out, had heard of and wanted to be in Miss Harriet's room.

The list of her students was called. I waited and waited and waited, but I didn't hear my name.

Miss Harriet's students lined up behind her, and I made a quick decision and lined up along with them. I didn't care what list I was on. I had been waiting three years to be in Miss Harriet's room and I was going to be in Miss Harriet's room. Period.

I took an empty desk in Miss Harriet's room, and in about a half hour the principal and my sister appeared in the doorway.

It had been discovered that I was missing from my assigned room, and it was feared that I had become lost en route. Since my sister was the only one who could identify me, she had to make the search with Miss Blankenship.

"There she is," my sister said.

She pointed. Everyone in the room turned to look at me.

I looked at my desk.

Miss Blankenship came over. She explained in a kind way how much I had worried everyone. This time she herself would accompany me to my room so I wouldn't get lost a second time.

I shook my head regretfully. "I want to be in Miss Harriet's room," I told my desk.

There was a silence.

I corrected my original statement. "I have to be in Miss Harriet's room."

The world stopped turning for a moment. It actually ground to a halt.

Then in this awesome silence, Miss Harriet said, "Oh, let her stay."

"If you're sure ... " the principal said. She sounded uncertain.

But Miss Harriet was not uncertain at all. "Yes, let her stay."

And with an audible click the world started up again.

That happened more than fifty years ago. Since that time, there have been lots of things in my life that I have looked forward to, only to have them turn out to be disappointments, things that never quite lived up to what I thought they would be, books that didn't turn out as I'd hoped, stories that ended up in the trash can.

But being in Miss Harriet's room was not one of life's disappointments. It was all I had dreamed.

And when I at last got to hear Miss Harriet read *The Adventures of Mabel,* it was better than anybody had ever read a book before or since.

Miss Harriet loved that book, and when she read it, every kid in the room—even the boys—became Mabel. *We* whistled the Lizard's Call. *We* communicated with wild animals. The frogs lined up on the bridge were there to warn *us* the bridge was about to collapse.

I didn't learn in first grade that I wanted to write books myself, but I did learn something that would prove true my whole life long—a good book, like *The Adventures of Mabel,* is well worth a three-year wait.

FOURTEEN

Satellite

"You want to buy a blacksnake?"

"What?"

"Do you want to buy a blacksnake?"

The boy was probably eleven years old, and he had knocked at the door of the log house. I don't get a lot of salespeople at the log house, so this was unusual.

And I had never had a snake salesperson ever.

The boy was standing on the porch, holding a pillowcase that contained a largish object. I felt somehow as if I were dealing with stolen goods.

"Where did you get this blacksnake?"

"Caught it."

"Where?"

He made a big gesture that included the land around the log house and the rest of the state of South Carolina.

I had, over the months, talked a lot about blacksnakes, asked a lot of questions about blacksnakes, stopped in the road to look at dead blacksnakes, warned workmen not to kill blacksnakes because it might be "my pet blacksnake."

An interest of this intensity doesn't go unnoticed in a rural community.

Also, a strange thing happens when I write a book. Things gravitate to me. Once I was starting a rodeo book, and some friends from Tucson called unexpectedly and invited Ed and I out to Rodeo Week.

Once I was writing about kids in foster homes, and I happened to sit by a woman on an airplane who was a foster parent. I picked her brain all the way to Chicago.

"You didn't catch it in my yard, did you?"

"I caught it in the woods."

"My woods?"

He shook his head.

"Can I see it?"

The boy hesitated. He opened a minute hole in the pillowcase and I peered in.

The snake lay in a dark, motionless heap at the bottom of the pillowcase. It was hard to judge its size.

It was the color of Moon. It could be Moon. This would explain a lot of things—including why I had not seen Moon in a couple of weeks—not since the day I had admired it after the rain.

"Is it alive?"

"Yes."

He held up the bag and poked it with one hand. The pillowcase writhed with sudden distaste.

I hesitated because I had never before thought to own a pillowcase with a snake inside. Still, if the snake inside happened to be Moon . . .

"How much?"

"Ten dollars."

"Ten dollars!"

"Yes, ten dollars." The boy's eyes narrowed. "I had a hard time catching this snake."

"But ten dollars . . . I don't know."

The silence hung in the air.

Striking a bargain is not one of my strong points; the best I can do is not give in too quickly. "Does that include the pillowcase?"

"No, it doesn't. I have to put this pillowcase back on my bed or my mom will want to know where it is."

I hesitated again, but not for long.

"Oh, all right. I'll take it."

"Where do you want me to put it?"

"I'll meet you down at the garage."

I went in the house and got a ten-dollar bill and met the boy at the garage. He asked again, "Where do you want me to put it?"

"How about in here."

I indicated a new plastic garbage can, and I took off the lid. The boy held the pillowcase over the garbage can and the snake slithered into the plastic garbage can and landed with a dull thud.

I looked in. The snake was in striking position, its tail vibrating.

I recalled my father's words. "When a snake wags its tail at you, it's not being friendly."

The snake lunged toward the top and I quickly put on the lid. We listened to the sounds of motion inside for a moment.

"I can get you another one. I can probably get as many as you want."

"This," I put my hand on the garbage can, "is all I want."

The mental image of that snake inside the garbage can coiled and ready to strike at the first opportunity was enough.

I waited until the boy had gone, and then I carried the garbage can around to the back of the house. I turned the can on its side and pried off the lid.

I stepped way back.

The snake took its time coming out, and not until it was stretched out full on the ground did I see that it wasn't Moon. This snake was slimmer, smaller, younger.

It headed for the nearest hiding place. This was a retaining wall made out of railroad ties.

The snake tried one crack between the railroad ties that didn't work out. It backed out with lightning speed. I recalled the not-so-charming story about the blacksnake who attacked the hunter out of frustration over just this very thing.

I stepped farther back.

The snake tried again. This crack wasn't right either.

It tried once again. This one worked, and the snake disappeared inside. This flurry of activity was accomplished in less time than it takes to tell about it.

I went out several times during the afternoon and the snake was still there. You wouldn't have known it unless you knew just what to look for, but there would always be a revealing bulge—like smooth black mortar squeezed between the railroad ties—that gave its presence away.

I expected the new blacksnake to be gone in the morning, and it was. But the next day it was back—apparently it liked the railroad ties. If it was going to stay around, I'd have to give it a name. I thought of Satellite.

I came to see Satellite fairly often. It tooled around a lot more than Moon, and I was always startling it or it was startling me. And neither of us particularly enjoyed being startled.

Satellite turned out to be a young skittish snake—without

Moon's maturity and coolness. It tended to panic if it saw me. But if I sat down on the railroad ties and just waited, eventually it would come out and not give me a glance.

Now my cup really runneth over, as they say. I had a front-yard blacksnake and a backyard blacksnake.

But my favorite was Moon.

FIFTEEN

Popcorn and Planes

When I was a little girl, my father used to take me to the airport on Saturdays to eat popcorn and watch the planes take off and land. I began to develop a lifelong love of flying then. I also developed a lifelong love of popcorn.

But I didn't have my first airplane ride until I was in college. During the summer before my senior year, I fell madly in love with Ed Byars. Ed was a college professor, a man of the world who had a yellow Mercury convertible and a 1931 Stinson airplane. He became my third lifelong love.

In our forty years of married life, Ed has owned about fifty airplanes, and I have owned one—a Cessna 152. And I have wanted to do a book about flying ever since I started writing.

Here's why I wanted to do it:

• I knew a lot about flying and airplanes, and no writer likes to see stuff like that go to waste.

• I loved flying, and writers like to write about the things that interest them.

Here's why I didn't do it:

• The only plot I could think of was something going wrong with the engine, the plane crashing, and the people having to survive. And I did not want to add to people's fear of flying. I wanted to make them love flying.

So even though I didn't have a plot, writing about flying was always in the back of my mind. Finally one day I got the germ of a plot: A crotchedy grandfather and his granddaughter have to fly across the country in an antique airplane.

I didn't know why they had to do it or what was going to happen to them, but those were mere details. I would figure all that out along the way.

I was pleased about doing a "journey" book. I got my start as a novelist with this kind of book—*Trouble River:* A crotchedy grandmother and her grandson have to go down Trouble River on a raft. It's the easiest kind of book to write, I think, because there's not much plot construction. All you need is a couple of characters, someplace they have to get to, and a bunch of interesting things that happen to them on the way.

That night I mentioned my idea to Ed. "What I'd like for you to do," I went on, "is to make out a route for the characters."

Within five minutes Ed had air maps spread out all over the floor. It turned out he'd been wanting to barnstorm across the country like this for a long time. I never had wanted to, but Ed convinced me with "If you're going to write about it, you've got to do it."

"All right," I said, "you'll be the crotchedy old grandfather and I'll be the young girl."

We set off in March in Ed's 1940 J-3 Piper Cub. The J-3 is a two place plane, one seat in front of the other, and I sat in front with a notepad on my lap, keeping a journal. Ed was in back, and behind him on the luggage rack was our dog Harvey.

The trip out took us seven days. That included about eight hours of flying per day—and so my 200-page notebook was full by the time we saw the Pacific Ocean. I tried to jot down little things that would bring back the trip to me when I was home facing the word processor.

Here are some sample entries:

• Day 1, March 11 . . . take off 8:36 A.M. . . . first stop Cornelius (2 hours, 3 minutes) . . . two airport dogs run out to meet us—one is three-legged. Inside the terminal, a cat jumps off the sofa and goes in the men's room . . . gas up (8.2 gallons 100LL) . . . take off . . . ceiling still 2000 feet . . .

• Day 2 . . . slow moving freight train—so slow I see how people used to jump aboard for a ride—kind of spur-of-the-moment thing my characters might have done if they lived by the tracks. Grandpa would only have to say, "All my life I've wanted to hop a train to California," and she would say, "Well, what's stopping us!" . . .

• Day 3 . . . wake up in motel at 6 A.M.—Ed has TV on, looking for weather info—instead we see a local story about Bimbo the Dancing Goat . . . dances to "Celebrations," 1-2-3 HOP . . . started dancing after his two kids were born . . . weather (finally) good . . .

• Day 4 . . . slower than usual . . . smoke on horizon shows we have a head wind . . . watch traffic on highway below—everything passes us but a motor home . . . we're doing about 45 mph . . .

• Day 5 . . . strong cross-wind . . . averaging 60 mph—take short-cut west of Deming (New Mexico)—beautiful, wild, remote country. Continental Divide along here somewhere . . . Call Lordsburg UNICOM radio—want to land on "Dirt-ruf" runway because of winds . . . land into wind—touchdown speed 10 mph . . . landing roll—less than 100 feet. When we turn onto taxi-way, I get out to hold wing . . .

• Day 6 . . . leave Blythe (California)—cut across Desert Center airstrip—ahead they've cut great steps out of the mountain . . . big pile of dirt beside it like something turned out of jello mold—we go over craggy mountain—rough air—scary! In valley beyond there is nothing—nobody—no tracks—not one single sign anybody's been here—awesome . . .

• Day 7 . . . land at Apple Valley—man with German accent directs us through Soledad Pass. "It's easy, I'll show you." "Wait, I'll get my map." "You don't need a map—just stay rrright of the mountains and take the second walley—not the walley the rrailroad goes through . . ."

. . . San Luis Obispo ahead . . . we're at 2100 feet now . . . last glimpse of Pacific through a gap in the hills . . . white plane ahead of us on final—we land, follow yellow line to Hangar marked Coastal Air . . .

Remember why I did this journal? Because a "journey" book was going to be easy and there wouldn't be a lot of plot construction? Well, after I finally, finally finished the manuscript and sent it to my publisher, they didn't like it. They said it didn't have enough plot construction.

I've now written the manuscript approximately seventeen times, and it still doesn't have enough plot construction. I'm not discouraged. I may get it on the eighteenth try. And if it never gets published, I'm still glad we did it.

And my lifelong loves continue to be flying, my husband . . . and popcorn.

SIXTEEN

A Few of My Favorite (and Unfavorite) Things

Here is the best thing about being a writer:

I am my own boss.

I work when I want to. If I don't feel like writing, I can go swimming or flying or jogging to Mexico. I can go on vacation when I want, and if I decide to take a month off, or a summer off, or a year off, I can do that, too.

I am the boss not only of my life, but of the book I'm writing. I can pick what I want to write about, and if it doesn't work out, I can pick something else. I can make the things happen that I want to happen. If characters die (as both Pap and Mud did in the early versions of *A Blossom Promise*), I can bring them back to life. I get a second chance and a third and a fourth. If it doesn't happen the way I want, I can do it over again and over again until it does.

Here is the worst thing about me being a writer:

I am a terrible boss. I have been that way all my life.

When I was little, my mother used to say, "Where are you going?"

"Outside."

"Not until you've done your homework."

"Mom, Wilma's waiting for me."

"Not until you've done your homework."

"Mommmmm . . ."

And I would do my homework.

Later it was "No talking on the phone until you've done your homework."

"Mom, I've got to tell Bunny something."

"You can tell her after you've done your homework."

"Mommmmm . . ."

"After you've done your homework."

Now, unfortunately, I am the only one around to force myself to write, and I am not a very forceful person.

Here are some of the ways I have used to get myself going. (Once I actually start writing, I'm all right—I really enjoy what I'm doing—it's just starting that's a problem for me.)

• I say, "Betsy, there is a writer in Kansas who is working on the exact same book that you are working on. A snake appeared on *her* front porch, and she also named it Moon, and this writer is not sitting on the sofa watching Road Runner cartoons like you're doing. She is at her word processor. And if you don't get up this minute and turn off the TV and start writing, you are going to open the newspaper one morning and see KANSAS WRITER WINS COVETED AWARD FOR SNAKE BOOK. And what are you going to do then?"

• I say, "Betsy, this Friday you're going on a trip, and when you come back from your trip, this same lousy manuscript is going to be sitting right here. And you know how you hate to come home to a lousy manuscript. Give yourself a break. Just rewrite the first chapter."

So I get the first chapter done, and the second and the third, until finally the manuscript is finished. Here's how it goes.

You finish a book, and you think it is the best book in the entire world, and you send it off to a publisher, and you get it back with a little printed slip of paper that says something like, "We're sorry, but this does not meet the needs of our list."

This hurts you a lot and, besides, you don't even know what "meet the needs of our list" means.

This "not meeting the needs of lists" goes on for a long time. Writing is like anything—baseball playing, piano playing, sewing, hammering nails. The more you work at it, the better you get. But it seems to take a longer time to get better at writing than hammering nails.

So, finally—and most people who want it badly enough and stick with it long enough do get published—you start getting letters that say something like, "We really like your manuscript, however all of us feel you have not quite reached your full potential."

So, finally, you do reach your full potential, and you can still get rejected (like my flying book). The good news is that being rejected doesn't hurt nearly as bad after you've published twenty books as it does when you're trying for your first.

The good things about writing far exceed the bad. You travel, you meet lots of nice people, and you get so much mail you have to get a huge mailbox. Here are a few of my favorite letters:

> Dear Betsy Byars,
>   All of us have to write to a real live author. Please write and tell me you're alive, or I will have to write a poem.

Dear Betsy,

Our class was trying to figure out how old you are, and we put down 1928 and under that 1990, and it came out you are 3918. Then we knew we had to subtract.

Dear Betsy,

I was reading THE BURNING QUESTIONS OF BINGO BROWN and I came to the word brassieres, and I didn't know what that was and I raised my hand and asked the teacher. You could have saved me a lot of embarrassment if you had just said bras.

Dear Betsy Byars,

I just have one question for you, and it's personal. Are you human?

Here's an unfavorite one:

Dear Betsy,

Our teacher wants us to do criticisms of the books we read. And here is my criticism. Your sentences are clogged.

I don't know exactly what clogged sentences are, but if they're anything like clogged drains, they're nothing to be proud of.

My favorite moment is probably this:

I get the galley proof sheets for my book, and I go over these very carefully. This is exactly the way the book will appear, and I don't want to have any mistakes. When I'm satisfied, I send the galleys back, and that's the last I see of it for a while.

Months pass. Sometimes I will see the jacket and sketches of the artwork, but sometimes I don't.

I never know my exact publication date—other than sometime in the spring or in the fall—until one day—sometime in the spring or in the fall—I go to my mailbox and see that I have a package.

I'm not a terribly cool person, so I rip it open in the driveway and there is my book.

It's a moment of absolute magic. It's as if I got an idea for a book that morning while I was brushing my teeth and now—presto!—here it is.

And all the work I did on the book—and there was work—disappears. And all the frustration—and there was that, too—disappears.

Everything disappears but this book. This is a real, honest-to-goodness book. And it's my book. I did this. There's my name.

It's a wonderful moment. I've published almost forty books now, and the magic is still there.

SEVENTEEN

A New Moon

The moment when I type a title page has been the same for most of my books—full of hope and enthusiasm and promise. But the ending is always different.

By the end of a book I have lived with the characters. Their joys have been mine. Their sorrows, too. I like these people. They're friends.

But I still have to let go.

Oh, once in a while it's a relief. I go, "Whew, I never thought I'd finish this in a hundred million years. I'm never going to write another book. It's a miracle it's over and I'm still reasonably sane."

But usually the "letting go" is more complicated than that.

Sometimes it's a long process. I step back like an artist, take a look, come back after a month or two for another look, read a review, come back for another look, read a letter from a reader, take another look . . .

And sometimes—with a favorite book like *The Midnight Fox*—I never let go. I will come across the book unexpectedly while cleaning a closet or a drawer and I'll say, "Oh, I haven't read this in a long time," and I'll sit down and read it! My own book! That I know every word of!

With *The Moon and I* I couldn't let go for a different reason. There was no ending. There couldn't be. Now, while I never type THE END when I finish a book, this time I *couldn't* type it. It wasn't finished.

I had seen Moon several times during the fall months. Each time the snake was lying on the warm stone in the fern bed or on the warm driveway. And each time I mentally said, "Goodnight, Moon. Sleep well."

I had read a lot about hibernation, and I could picture Moon curled beneath the earth—heartbeat, breathing, and growth all slowed almost to the point of stopping, barely alive.

I even occasionally envisioned Moon twisted with other snakes in one of those balls of snakes that are so entwined that when they come out of hibernation, they do it together, and actually roll down the hill for a few feet.

I had a harder time picturing Moon with other creatures— frogs and turtles, even mice, although I had read that this happens.

But hibernation is not the end. It's just an intermission. And I'm not the kind of person who would ever leave something at intermission. I want to see the end.

And then one morning exactly a month after I had last seen Moon, I went to a pet shop. My dog Harvey's birthday was coming up—he was going to be eleven—and I wanted to get him something especially nice.

I selected a squeaky rubber hot dog and a chew stick. While

the clerk was gift-wrapping them for me, I walked back to look at the parrots.

As I expected, all the parrots had signs on their stands saying I might bite. Might? They were almost falling off their perches to get to me.

I turned around.

Then I saw—in an alcove behind the parrots, among the hamsters and gerbils—a snake.

"I didn't know you had any snakes," I said.

"We just have two—the speckled king snake and the baby boa."

The baby boa was an unappealing dark lump in one corner of its cage. The price was also unappealing—$139.

But the speckled king snake! The speckled king snake was beautiful—black with little paint dabs of pale yellow all over it. The throat was creamy yellow, too.

And the speckled king snake wasn't just lying there in a blob like the baby boa. It was busy working its way up the glass side of its aquarium. It was involved in its universe.

I walked closer.

The snake got to the top of the aquarium and slid onto the screen that kept it from sliding on out. It clung to the screen, moving slowly across.

The snake got about halfway across the screen and then plopped down onto the floor of the cage. Then it nosed around the water bowl, sticking its tongue out a time or two.

The snake was about two feet long—the perfect length for a snake—and about as big around as my finger—the perfect width.

And it had a small smile on its face!

I was enchanted. I wanted to take this snake home with me then and there.

My brain began to perk. I could keep it over the winter—I

could let it go in the spring! I could set this beautiful snake free!

"Are king snakes native to this area?" I asked. I know you're not supposed to let anything out into an unnatural habitat.

I had read a sobering tale about Pacific islanders who had imported a couple of mongooses to help with the snake population, and after the mongooses got finished with all the snakes, they started on the chickens and anything else that moved.

"I think so. I'll check."

The clerk went to the front of the pet shop to check it out in one of her "Getting to Know Snakes" books. I stayed watching the snake.

She came back. "Yes."

"And how often do you have to feed it?"

"Oh, once or twice a month."

"What does it eat?" I could see that there was a tiny goldfish swimming around in the water bowl. "Goldfish?"

That would be easy enough. I knew boas had to have little baby pigs and rabbits.

"He has eaten goldfish. We had a garter snake in here last spring and it wouldn't eat anything else. We give this snake a small mouse every two weeks as well."

"A live one?"

"Yes."

That wouldn't be as easy as dropping a small goldfish in a bowl of water, but it would be a lot easier than a piglet.

"A mouse like these?" I pointed to a cage of active hamsters. It was hard for me to imagine the graceful snake above wanting to eat one.

"Oh, no, much smaller. We keep the small mice in the back. You put the mouse in the cage, and if the snake doesn't eat it right away, you take the mouse out. Otherwise the mouse is liable to bite the snake and hurt it."

"Ah . . ."

I knew I wouldn't be much better at handling mice than I had been at handling snakes. But I could learn.

"Can you pick it up? Does it strike?"

"Well, we advise people to use light gloves at first until the snake has a chance to get used to them, but the bite is a mere scratch."

"I know ... I've had one of those before."

There was a pause.

The clerk looked me over. Apparently I didn't look like the usual snake customer because she said, "Were you thinking of getting the snake for yourself?"

I hesitated.

"Well, I have four grandsons," I began, and then I came out with the truth.

"Yes, it's for me."

I waited to see if I was going to feel foolish, but I didn't.

I kept standing there, silently arguing with myself. The adult in me was saying, "Betsy, you have no need for a snake. It is absolutely ridiculous for you to have a snake."

The child in me was saying, "Listen, I've wanted a snake all my life and I don't care what you say. It's been on my list since I was 7 years old and I didn't get the horses and I didn't get the goat like Buttsy and I'm going to have this snake. So there! Nyah!"

Then I remembered that the real reason I had wanted to grow up, the main reason I had been willing to even consider becoming an adult, was so I could have as many pets as I wanted.

What is the point of being an adult and having to act like one if you don't take advantage of it?

So I said the words I knew I was going to say the moment I first saw the snake.

"I'll take it. Wrap it up."

EIGHTEEN

The Beginning

I was a happy woman.

I drove home with an aquarium and a screen cover and a heating pad and two bags of corncob bedding and a small pet pen (in which I would put the lizards I would catch) and a drinking dish and a small goldfish on the backseat of the car.

The snake, tied into a muslin bag, was beside me on the front seat. The bag writhed the whole way home as the snake tried to deal with being tied up in a muslin bag. Its positions varied from roller-coasterlike loops to coiled lumps to long-searching stretches.

The snake books had all suggested that beginners start with garter snakes because they eat earthworms and goldfish. But I had fallen for a speckled king snake, and nothing else would do.

King snakes have everything going for them. They are hardy

in captivity and very handsome snakes. Some—like mine—are even beautiful.

I braked at a stop sign and looked down at the bag. It shifted so that the knot was pointing upward. Then it shifted again and tipped sideways.

I had no idea that a muslin bag could be so endlessly fascinating!

But then this bag contained a miracle of nature, a natural phenomenon.

As I watched, I felt a rush of pleasure as sharp as I had had as a girl when I peered into my mayonnaise jar and watched the bullsnake poking its head out of the egg.

I put my hand beneath the bag and felt the incredible lightness of the snake, the quickness. It was like a miracle tied up in a muslin bag—a rope come to life.

The light changed to green, but I didn't notice. The car behind me honked.

I glanced in the rearview mirror. I wanted to roll down the window and call to the man in the Toyota, "Sorry! See, I just got this snake? And it's tied up in a bag? And I was holding the bag and—listen, have you ever held a snake in a bag before? It's incredible! Wait a minute. This is something you have to feel to experience. Everyone ought to have the experience of holding a snake in a bag. You are not going to believe how great this is!"

Instead I put the bag down on the seat and pressed down on the gas pedal.

As I drove through the intersection, my mind began to perk.

With this snake, I'll get to see it eat! I'll get to see it shed its skin! I'll get to see all the things I didn't get to see with Moon!

Of course, I couldn't do a book about this snake because I was just going to keep it in its cage. Nothing was going to happen to write about.

I had no idea that within a month—on Thanksgiving Day—the snake would escape its cage, crawl into the back burner of the stove, and when I turned on the oven to cook the turkey, the snake would come crawling out—fast.

A snake's business, apparently, is to be able to get in and out of difficult places, and so by nature it's an escape artist.

I had no idea that two months after the stove incident, the snake would escape again. This time it would hide under the VCR and come out while I was watching *Swan Lake*. My husband later said that was the highest leap he'd ever seen in a ballet.

"The snake's?" I asked.

"No, yours."

Anyway, I didn't want to do another snake book—one is enough.

Still—all the same—it wouldn't hurt to type out a quick title page when I got home.

A SNAKE NAMED FRECKLES
by
Betsy Byars

PUBLISHED WORKS

1962   *Clementine* (illustrated by Charles Wilton), Houghton
        Mifflin.

1965   *The Dancing Camel* (illustrated by Harold Berson),
        Viking.

1966   *Rama, the Gypsy Cat* (illustrated by Peggy Bacon),
        Viking.

1967   *The Groober* (illustrated by Betsy Byars), Harper.

1968   *The Midnight Fox* (illustrated by Ann Grifalconi),
        Viking.

1969   *Trouble River* (illustrated by Rocco Negri), Viking.

1970   *The Summer of the Swans* (illustrated by Ted
        CoConis), Viking.

1971   *Go and Hush the Baby,* (illustrated by Emily A.
        McCully), Viking.

1972   *The House of Wings* (illustrated by Daniel Schwartz),
        Viking.

1973   *The Winged Colt of Casa Mia* (illustrated by Richard
        Cuffari), Viking.

1973   *The 18th Emergency* (illustrated by Robert
        Grossman), Viking.

1974   *After the Goat Man* (illustrated by Ronald Himler),
        Viking.

1975   *The Lace Snail* (illustrated by Betsy Byars), Viking.

1976   *The TV Kid* (illustrated by Richard Cuffari), Viking.

1977   *The Pinballs,* Harper.

1978   *The Cartoonist* (illustrated by Richard Cuffari),
        Viking.

1979   *Goodbye, Chicken Little,* Harper.

1980   *The Night Swimmers* (illustrated by Troy Howell),
        Delacorte.

1981   *The Cybil War* (illustrated by Gail Owens), Viking.

1982   *The Animal, the Vegetable, and John D. Jones*
        (illustrated by Ruth Sanderson), Delacorte.

1982   *The 2000-Pound Goldfish,* Harper.

1983   *The Glory Girl,* Viking.

1984   *The Computer Nut* (illustrated by Guy Byars),
        Viking.

1985   *Cracker Jackson,* Viking.

1985   *The Golly Sisters Go West* (illustrated by Sue
        Truesdale), Harper.

1986   *The Not-Just-Anybody Family* (illustrated by
        Jacqueline Rogers), Delacorte.

1986   *The Blossoms Meet the Vulture Lady* (illustrated by
        Jacqueline Rogers), Delacorte.

1987   *The Blossoms and the Green Phantom* (illustrated by
        Jacqueline Rogers), Delacorte.

1987   *A Blossom Promise* (illustrated by Jacqueline
        Rogers), Delacorte.

1988   *The Burning Questions of Bingo Brown* (illustrated
        by Cathy Bobak), Viking.

1988   *Beans on the Roof* (illustrated by Melodye Rosales),
        Delacorte.

1989   *Bingo Brown and the Language of Love* (illustrated
        by Cathy Bobak), Viking.

1990   *Bingo Brown, Gypsy Lover* (illustrated by Cathy
        Bobak), Viking.

1990   *Hooray for the Golly Sisters* (illustrated by Sue
        Truesdale), Harper.

1991   *The Seven Treasure Hunts* (illustrated by Jennifer
        Barrett), Harper.

1991   *Wanted . . . Mud Blossom* (illustrated by Jacqueline
        Rogers), Delacorte.